Wake Up to Wealth

D1557868

Wake Up
to Wealth

Bob Mandel

CELESTIAL ARTS
BERKELEY, CALIFORNIA

Acknowledgments

Many wonderful people have influenced my writing this book, including my wife Mallie, without whose support I might never have completed it, and my business partner Sondra Ray, without whose inspiration I might never have started it. I also wish to thank the following people whose teachings and writings have helped shape my own thinking: Dr. Deepak Chopra, Dr. Tom Verney, Leonard Orr, Phil Laut, Rev. Ike, Steven Covey, Jim Autry, Robert Bly, Fred Lehrman, and Patrick Collard. Finally, I want to express my gratitude to my lifelong friend, George Bequary, who in winning the lottery, proved to me once again that wealth is truly a state of mind.

Cover and text design by Sarah Levin

First Printing, 1994

Library of Congress Cataloging-in-Publication Data:
Mandel, Robert Steven, 1943-
   Wake up to wealth / by Bob Mandel.
     p. cm.
   ISBN 0-89087-709-2
   1. Wealth. 2. Wealth—Psychological aspects. I. Title.
HB251.M3 1994   93-38528
   332. 024—dc20   CIP

1 2 3 4 5 6 / 99 98 97 96 95 94

Contents

*I dedicate this book to my grandchildren, Ariana and Sam,
who I pray will live in a world of peace and prosperity.*

What Is Wealth?

According to Webster, "wealth" originated from the Middle English word *wele* which became *weal,* meaning "a sound, healthy, or prosperous state: well-being." The word "commonwealth" grew out of *commonweal,* a pleasing pun when you think about it.

Webster defines wealth as an "abundance of valuable material possessions or resources; abundant supply; profusion; all property that has a money value; all material objects that have economic utility, especially the stock of useful goods having economic value in existence at any one time."

Wealth, as a word, undergoes a peculiar evolution—from a state of health, well-being, and common good to one of temporary material possessions, accumulated money, and individual proprietorship. In one sense, we might say that the rise of capitalism coincided with the decline of the true meaning of wealth, a bold statement perhaps, but one which merits contemplation given the current eco-financial crisis.

What is wealth? Clearly, it is a state of abundance. But abundance of what? We can harness a wealth of information, a wealth of experience, a wealth of love and a wealth of energy. On the other hand, we might accumulate a wealth of struggle, a wealth of conflict, a wealth of confusion or, worse, a wealth of scarcity.

We can experience a wealth of good times or a wealth of hard times, a wealth of friends or a wealth of loneliness, a wealth of responsibilities or a wealth of freedom.

In other words, we can apply the principle of abundance to anything we value, consciously or unconsciously priming the pump of our own personal fortunes, whether positive or negative.

How often do we hear the story of a fabulously successful businessperson who, sinking into spiritual bankruptcy, seeks out a different treasure from life? Not that often? Often enough, I suggest, and more often every day. For, to paraphrase a biblical proverb, what is the bottom line profit of amassing a huge personal fortune when the price we pay is our very souls? Is that financial freedom?

On the other hand, to deny the material kingdom and blindly crusade through life thinking that sacrifice, struggle, and scarcity will automatically open the gates of heaven demonstrates a profound lack of spiritual wisdom, not to mention common sense. Surely, poverty is not the soil of the good life any more than money is the root of all evil.

This book is about how to have our cake and eat it, too. But first we must know what sort of cake we truly desire. We want to be sure that this cake will nurture us inside and out. And we don't want hand-me-down recipes for cakes that taste good at first bite but leave an aftertaste in our mouths and an emptiness in our guts.

No, true wealth is primarily health, and health is spiritual, mental, and physical. And true wealth is commonwealth, which means a flourishing global village.

Earth is a family business. The creation of commonwealth can be a labor of love for all of us. Abundance is there for the taking, but taking implies giving value in return. The art of giving and receiving is ultimately an act of love, whether applied to personal or business relationships. All relationships are personal. We are colleagues, custodians, and caretakers of each other and our living planet.

The universe is unlimited. Only our minds set limits, and where our minds lack imagination our lives become depleted. Then we struggle to conquer, divide, and accumulate the most meaningless things we can at other people's expense. Not to mention the cost to Mother Earth herself, which, if she continues to cough up at the current rate, will choke all hope for survival.

It's a Catch-22. It's a global death-urge masquerading as survival of the financially fittest. It's time to bury the Darwinian-Marxist concept of life, an obsolete concept at best. It's time to let go of the image of Kruschev pounding his shoe on the table, boasting, "We will bury you." Did he mean militarily or economically? In the end, communism destroyed itself. Capitalism will destroy all of us unless we resurrect the true meaning of wealth.

The universe is infinite and we have the potential to access its abundance if we think correctly. If we continue to think incorrectly, however, we will divide and conquer and inevitably march toward oblivion, millionaire soldier ants swept off the precarious cliff of life. The planet is a spaceship traveling through time and space; we must correct its course by correcting our consciousness.

Wake up to wealth, I say...personal wealth and common-wealth—spiritual, mental, and physical well-being.

We live at the centerpoint of all time and space, which stretches out infinitely—in all dimensions and directions—from the core of our beings. We are the pivotal point from which all abundance circulates.

The wealth we need to wake up to is quantum wealth, a far cry from the linear struggle to make ends meet and the equally fatal attraction for accumulating the most toys before we die.

We need to be born-again commonwealthy, each of us spinning his or her own unique wheel of success which, in turn, sets others' wheels in motion. Like a perfect timepiece, we can be a perfect wealthpiece. And the pendulum of prosperity can swing for us all.

"You can go to the ocean with a teaspoon or a bucket, the ocean doesn't care."

Rev. Ike

Chapter 1

The Legend of the Sleeping Giant

*O*nce there was a Sleeping Giant. He slept in a high mountain valley, just over the hill from a small, quiet village. The villagers knew of this huge Being. Often, they would hear Him roll over in His endless sleep—causing buildings to shake and windows to shatter—or roar if He had a bad dream, sending a terrible shudder down their spines. But this was a village of little people, and few of them had the magnitude or fortitude to venture near the Sleeping Giant. In fact, even though He slept just over the nearest hill, very few, if any, of the villagers, their parents, or their grandparents had ever seen the Great Sleeping One.

Of course, as usual in stories such as this, there were many legends about the Sleeping Giant. Although no one knew for sure if any of them had actually seen the Giant, the elders of the village claimed they had in their youth, and they argued amongst themselves about whether He was a good giant who protected the village or a bad giant who, when awakened, would subjugate all the villagers. One elder "remembered" when the Giant first arrived. He said that the village was extremely wealthy at that time, unlike now, a time of great scarcity and struggle. "This was a village of the rich men only. Everyone had more gold than they could possibly use," the elder recalled. But then the Giant appeared. He demanded that all the gold be gathered and placed in a cave over the hill. When this was done, the Giant said He was tired and would take a nap, and no one should awaken Him if they valued their gold or their lives.

Another elder begged to disagree. Every day in the town square cafe, these two elders would debate the village past while other villagers looked on, some with their own variations of these legends.

According to this second elder, the first elder's memory was totally unreliable. The truth was, yes, the village was once extremely wealthy, and, yes, the villagers stored their gold in a cave over the hill. Then one day a kind Giant appeared and said that He could teach them how to be Giants, too. For a while the lessons were successful, and some of the little villagers grew bigger. But then the ones that remained little or could not learn their lessons became jealous, and the villagers began to fight among themselves as never before. Finally, one day, after a big villager murdered a little villager, the kind Giant shouted, "STOP!" so loud that all the villagers heard a ringing in their ears for some time to come. Suddenly, all the villagers who had grown big were little again. Then the kind Giant announced that He was going to sleep in the next valley beside the cave and would not wake up and teach them until they stopped fighting and prayed for forgiveness. He said that if anyone tried to wake Him before there was peace in the village, He would leave and never return. The Giant went to sleep. The villagers didn't know what to do: they loved the Giant and wanted to learn His lessons. They didn't want Him to leave yet they couldn't stop fighting amongst themselves. The more they fought, the more frightened they grew.

Their fear gave birth to the idea that the Sleeping Giant had stolen their gold and there was no way to retrieve it from the cave where He slept.

There was a third elder who laughed and said there was no Sleeping Giant at all. He claimed that the villagers were victims of a collective delusion. But nobody seemed interested in this point of view.

The children listened to these tales which kindled their curiosity and aroused their vivid imaginations. They yearned to see the Sleeping Giant but were strictly forbidden to do so by their parents.

Hard times had gripped the small village. Life had become a matter of struggle, endurance, poverty, and either outbursts of conflict or silent misery. The more the children observed their parents' hardship, the more they became determined to do something. And that something took the shape of the Sleeping Giant.

One day after school the children disappeared into the mountain valley where the Sleeping Giant slept by the cave filled with gold. As they approached the Great One, they debated among themselves what action, if any, to take. One boy urged the group to turn back, reminding his friends of the legend of the Sleeping Giant's enormous might and meanness. Another child, a small girl, said, no, they should awaken the mighty Giant, arguing that perhaps He would deliver their parents from the plight of poverty, struggle, and unhappiness.

Most of the children felt trapped in the middle, fear and worry shaking their knees, awe and wonder tickling their fancies.

The children approached and beheld the Sleeping Giant. He was far bigger than they had ever imagined. It took all the children of the village, nearly one hundred of them, to surround the Giant's great body. The children instinctively held hands and stood in silence, not knowing what to do next.

Back in the village, the parents had noticed that their children had vanished, and although they suspected the worst, they were still too frightened to go after them. They gathered in their place of prayer and asked God to return their offspring safely and speedily. One by one, all of the villagers fell to their knees, weeping from the depth of their littleness in hopes that their children might be delivered without harm. And yet, not one of these little people dared to venture forth from the security of the little village, despite their misery, scarcity, struggle, and unhappiness.

The children stood near the Sleeping Giant, paralyzed by their fear and the fear of their parents. Nevertheless, one brave girl poked the huge Sleeping One with a stick, and soon all the other children joined in. The children then recited in unison:

> Wake up Giant,
> Wake up Giant,
> Wake up from your endless dream.
> Open your eyes,
> Awaken and rise,
> And please, don't be mean.

And still the Giant slept.

The children proceeded to climb upon the Sleeping Giant's huge sprawled-out body. Despite their trepidation, they lunged forward as if propelled by a force even greater than the Giant Himself. Finally, the Great One stirred under the pressure of this mighty collective innocence. The children took a huge deep breath and bellowed in unison from the fullness of their little lungs, "WE DEMAND YOUR GREAT AWAKENING!"

The mountains roared, the hills rolled, and the valley of the Sleeping Giant heaved back and forth in all its majesty. Back in the village, buildings shook and windows shattered. It seemed as if a giant earthquake had struck, like the end of the world was near, and all the little villagers scurried like squirrels for safety, frightened for their lives and the lives of their lost children.

As the Giant sat up, the children moved off His body, but did not run away. The Giant gently rubbed His eyes. He yawned a yawn that echoed throughout the hills. Then He looked at all the children and the biggest smile in the world spread across His huge face. Quietly He said to them, "I am yours. You are mine." He stretched out His huge arms in magnitude and love, His fingers unfurling tender tentacles.

The awakened Giant took a giant inhale and slowly exhaled, His breath creating a gentle, loving windswirl which lifted the children and twisted them in circles of sweetbreeze—whirlwinds of gentle love. As they turned, they grew, and as they grew, they turned, spinning from littleness into magnitude in a few, short seconds. And when the Giant let them drop, they were no longer little children, but were giants themselves, His very equals in size, shape, and strength.

The now big Children were astounded by their transformation. The formerly Sleeping Giant arose and embraced the giant children one by one. Then He took them into the secret cave where the gold had been hidden for so many years. The children entered the darkness of the cave, but when they focused their eyes they beheld the brilliant, blinding light. Gold, diamonds, emeralds, sapphires—a technicolor treasure chest of infinite abundance.

Meanwhile, the villagers gathered in the town square. They sensed that a great change had occurred, but no one could express it until suddenly, in an instant, they experienced that fear had left their hearts and love had replaced this fear, and that in this love was joy and peace and faith in the future. No worries, they thought simultaneously. They were tempted to discuss and debate the change that had occurred, but instead they all began to smile, giggle, then guffaw.

Their laughter was abruptly interrupted by a stupendous sound, a loud thumping noise marching towards them from the hills. They looked at the crest of the hill and saw an army of giants standing in unison.

The children gazed at their little village and their shocked little parents, and it seemed to them like a tiny town of ants. They inhaled, as the Sleeping Giant had taught them, and gently breathed a swirling breeze down towards the village. Their parents were swept into the air, as They had been before, magical tornadoes twisting and turning from littleness to magnitude in a few, short, windy seconds. And when the parents looked up again, they recognized their children and ran towards them in joy and tears to embrace their saviors.

After explaining what had happened, the children took their parents to the Valley of the Sleeping Giant. As they neared the place where the Giant slept, they realized that He was gone. They searched everywhere, but there was no sign of the good Giant.

Finally, they led their parents into the cave where the town's gold and jewels glittered brilliantly. And there, lying in the middle of this gigantic, golden glow was a radiant newborn baby, fast asleep, with the sweetest little smile on his face.

◆ *Chapter 2* ◆

Walking in the Big Sleep

*I*f we want to wake up to true wealth, the story of the
Sleeping Giant can provide valuable lessons. Primarily, it
says that we, like the Giant, are asleep. If we don't recognize
that we're asleep, how can we ever awaken?

What does it mean that we're asleep? It means that we're unconscious and that we're dreaming. We're unconscious because
our reality is distorted by perceptions and sensations of a limited
consciousness. We are trapped in a world we have imagined, a
world of suffering, struggle, and scarcity. This world is like a
movie; and we are sleepwalkers in a dream. Each of us is both the
dreamer and the dreamed.

The problem is, we think it's real. It certainly looks real, feels
real, smells real, tastes real, and sounds real. It seems scientifi-
cally measurable and governed by natural laws. Of course, there
are always the interesting exceptions and questions. If a tree falls
in the forest and nobody's there, does it make a crashing sound?

The more we have learned about the nature of reality, the
more we have revised our definition of reality. Before Copernicus,
reality was that Earth was the center of the Solar System. Before

quantum physics, reality was linear, time and space clearly separate dimensions. Our reality is rapidly changing with computers, satellites, and intergalactic telescopes feeding us more information every day. But what if the very reality we are investigating is not the real thing at all? What if it's just a figment of our imagination, a collective hallucination, culturally-induced and passed down from generation to generation. What if we're dreaming?

The Sleeping Giant rests by a cave of enormous wealth. Meanwhile, the village people struggle and suffer. The cave is both the reality we've hidden from our consciousness and the wealth we seek to acquire. There is no difference. Plato's allegory of the cave is a story about reality and illusion. We live in the shadow of scarcity while true wealth remains buried in the darkness.

We fear the darkness. When we were children, we slept with the light on. Nighttime is the time for demons, goblins, and bogeymen. We feel safer in daylight. If we never explore the darkness, however, we never discover the hidden treasure.

The Giant sleeps by the cave of endless wealth. Is He the guardian of the treasure and the town or is he the enemy? It's interesting, too, that it is questionable whether anyone has ever seen the Giant though many claim to remember His arrival. What's clear is that these little villagers are spiritually bankrupt, cowardly complainers who would rather talk about the problem than investigate a solution. They are great storytellers, but hardly people of action.

The first elder tells the story of an evil Giant who conquers and plunders and then sleeps. This represents one view of history, to be sure. According to this perspective, the past is largely a succession of atrocities which we must remember or we are destined to repeat them. The Giant represents power and power corrupts.

Here is a group of people who have fantasized a monster as an excuse for not exploring the dark cave where their treasure awaits them. They are dreamers. They love to dwell on the past or focus on the future, but when it comes to the present, they are hopeless. They always have excuses for not taking action. And the root of inaction is fear, which when indulged, engenders paralysis. The Giant is a symbol of fear, a big bully who steals our gold, won't let us have our way, and who, even when asleep, sends shudders through our spines. He is the incarnation of the fear that subjugates us.

According to the second elder, however, the Giant is a benevolent fellow and a spiritual teacher. In this version of the story, the villagers store their treasure in the cave before the Giant appears. Why would they do that? Why didn't they put their wealth under their mattresses or buy stocks or mutual funds? And why does the Giant appear after they hide their gold in the cave?

Clearly, these villagers once had a true sense of commonwealth. They didn't hoard their separate riches; rather, they pooled their wealth. Why did they hide it in the dark cave? Obviously, they were concerned and wanted to make sure their treasure was safe. It's important to note that this slight fear existed prior to the Giant's arrival. The Giant entered the scene after the villagers pooled their wealth, a spiritual master ready to take His students to the next level. His lessons worked to an extent, but, ultimately, He could not lead His students beyond their own willingness. This tells us that growth is a function of individual free will and cannot be imposed from the outside. Otherwise, the Giant could have zapped the entire village, and made everyone a giant.

Continuing the second elder's story, some villagers learned their lessons and grew bigger, but others lagged behind. What's interesting here is that even the ones that grew bigger did not become giants, implying that our growth is somehow interconnected and that no one can totally evolve without everyone doing so.

Jealousy, conflict, and finally, murder entered the previously peaceful village. We might wonder, well, didn't the Giant know this would happen? What kind of Giant is He, anyway, if He could not foresee such an occurrence? It's the age-old question, how could God create a world that is filled with so much pain and suffering? The answer is He didn't. Neither the Giant nor God created inequality, competition, and war. We are created with free will, one of our most precious possessions, indeed. It is we who create the nightmare of envy, jealousy, and revenge when we forget who we are and make choices based on fear.

The Giant merely instructed His students. The villagers, already afraid as evidenced by hiding their wealth in the cave, could not cope with the apparent disparity in their growth. When the ones who remained little observed the ones who grew, their fear was activated and they, at that moment, fell from grace, believed themselves separate and deprived of a special blessing. They strayed from the path once they thought they were less, which inevitably resulted in crime and punishment.

Here we learn the folly of envy. When we resent those who have more than we do, our resentment keeps us from having the very things we want. When we resent the rich, we are actually rejecting the part of ourselves that is rich. The alternative is to rub shoulders with them and let that golden touch rub off on us. Or we can study the belief systems of the wealthy and integrate them into our lives. Often, the rich will share their ideas freely; they are generous with their knowledge.

The Giant put an end to havoc, at least temporarily, according to the second elder. He reduced everyone to size and announced that He would sleep by the cave until the villagers stopped fighting and prayed for forgiveness. With the Giant asleep, the villagers didn't know what to do. Why not? The Giant had told them what to do. Obviously, they knew what to do and chose not to, continuing their pattern of dispute and conflict. Their fighting lead to increased fear which, in turn, spawned the myth of the evil Giant.

Why did the Giant sleep—and why by the cave? Clearly He decided to sleep until the villagers awakened from their dream of conflict. And His bed was by the cave to symbolize that the villagers could reclaim their magnificent commonwealth when they awakened to their personal magnificence. And they could not awaken to their personal magnificence until they healed their relationships through prayer and forgiveness.

"Hard times gripped the village." The fall from grace is the descent into purgatory, which is the consequence of thinking we are sinners. Until we are forgiven, we remain in a state of separation from grace, doomed to struggle and poverty.

And then along came the children. The children must be the ones who save the day. They not only represent the innocence that must be reclaimed before true wealth can be attained; they are also symbolic of the inner child. The parents are emotionally crippled and mentally disturbed. There can be no healing without the heart of a child.

The children embark on their adventure after school. They are the true students, unlike their parents who failed to learn their lessons.

Of course, the children love their parents and are motivated by their desire to save them. As Gurdjieff said, "All children want to take their parents to heaven." At first the children, much like their parents, argue amongst themselves whether the Giant is good or bad. Children learn from imitation. They are born mimics. They learn how to relate to each other by observing their role models. Naturally, the children copy their parents and dispute the Giant as did their elders.

It is a young girl who leads the way. The feminine is the capacity to receive, which is what is needed here.

All one hundred children surround the Giant in a circle and hold hands. The circle represents the unity of consciousness that is required to confront the Giant. The children know this instinctively. Their parents knew this once when they formed the commonwealth, but they have long since forgotten.

Indeed, so frightened are the villagers that even when they

realize that their children are gone, they cannot take action. At least they pray, which the Giant had requested, presumably a long time ago. They fall to their knees, but they stay there. The children sense their parents' paralysis and chant. Perhaps they realize that it is not the Giant they need to wake up, but their parents.

The children, again led by the little girl, begin to poke the Giant. Then they "fear forward," propelled by a force greater than the Giant, climbing upon His slumbering body and demanding, in unison, His great awakening.

"Fearing forward" is an important concept. Fear can be a red light or a green light, and if we mistake one for the other we are in trouble. In this case, fear is obviously a green light, an invitation to more abundance and excitement. The children recognize their fear as an ally and proceed to take action. Not only do they have the courage to climb the Giant's body, establishing a greater connection with Him; they DEMAND His awakening. They know that their word is law in the universe; they already possess the power they seek from the Giant.

The children are propelled by a force greater than the Giant, an important point. They are aware that the source of power is not in an idol or demigod, but in themselves. We can each tap this force for our individual and collective betterment, but we can neither contain nor possess it. It's bigger than all of us, even giants. The Giant is thus reduced to His appropriate role, an example of the way but not the way itself. Your higher self can lead you to your guru, but a true guru always leads you back to your higher self.

The earth rumbles, the Giant wakes up, and what does He do? He yawns, smiles and quietly tells them, "I am yours. You are mine." Then He lovingly extends His arms to them. The Giant is powerful, but gentle, wise, and happy. His yawn is a taking in of new air, new life—renewal, rebirth. His smile indicates the joy of awakening. He belongs to the children and the children belong to

Him because there is no separation between His giantness and their innocence. They have undergone their rite of passage.

The Giant inhales and exhales, demonstrating the power of the breath of life. The children are transformed into giants. Releasing their fear of the Giant; having the courage to approach, touch, and stand on him; and then demanding that He awaken, the children have reclaimed their own magnitude.

Meanwhile, in the village, the parents detect a shift. The fear in their hearts has been released. They are tempted to discuss and debate but, instead, they laugh. Laughter is the therapy the villagers needed. They are now lighthearted. The inner child has been healed. They still don't know what has transpired, but their trust in life has been resurrected.

The children, now giants, complete the healing of their parents by transforming them into giants, as well. This can be accomplished in unison because fear has departed and the feeling of commonwealth has returned. Now everyone can be equal, parent and child, villager and villager.

When the children lead their parents to the Valley of the Giant, He is no longer sleeping outside the cave. He is now a radiant, newborn baby, lying on the village treasure, with "the sweetest smile on His face." This evokes the symbol of the baby Jesus, transferred from the manger to the cave, from poverty to wealth.

We can have it all once we release our fear, trust our children, and allow the child within us to lead the way to our true magnificence. We can wake up to wealth, but first we have to acknowledge that we are asleep.

Chapter 3

Envision Endless Wealth

W e're all dreamers. Perhaps we're all alike in our unconsciousness...the proverbial human condition. Sometimes, however, we have glimpses of the other side of the mirror. We have mystical experiences, breakthrough experiences. We also have the capacity to create. Our minds can imagine things that seem to transcend our limited reality. We create legends, myths, art, music, dance, theatre. We also create ideas. We have inspirations, sparks of creative energy that ignite our imaginations and empower our activities.

We have visions, too. Sometimes they happen spontaneously, sometimes we make them up. But we are visionaries in the sense that we see things with our minds' eyes. We often think of a visionary as someone who sees the future, events that have not yet taken place. But to the visionary, there is no time, no future to be seen. The visionary sees what he or she sees now. He or she is tapping into a source of sight that enables him or her to transcend linear time and linear thinking. The visionary takes quantum leaps. Although the visionary still lives within the dream, he or she sees as if temporarily awake.

I often ask myself, what can we do within the dream to open our eyes to true wealth? How can we move from unconsciousness to consciousness? I think we must begin by creating a vision of an alternative reality. Secondly, we must examine the nature of the dream and the dreamer so we know what and who we're dealing with. Then, and only then can we gather the tools, supplies, and resources we need to build the bridge to true wealth.

If all we did was to study the dream, we'd be trapped in the darkness. No, we can't find the light by investigating the darkness alone. If the Sleeping Giant never awakened, if we didn't have a vision of the waking state, the story would go nowhere. So it behooves us to develop a vision of endless wealth before we begin to examine the mechanics of dreaming and the work of waking up. Before we build the bridge, we must envision where we're going. Otherwise, we could build a bridge to nowhere.

So, let's begin with something big...the universe. How do you see it? If we were asked this question before the late seventeenth century, our answer would have been quite different. We would have seen ourselves as the center of the universe, our home planet, Earth, the center of the Solar System. Now we know better, or do we?

We "know" that we do not live at the center of things, that even our solar system is one of countless solar systems inhabiting a universe which probably has neither a beginning nor an end.

Think of the universe. How vast can you imagine it? When I visualize it, I feel like an astronaut traveling in space. I voyage to the moon and peer back at Earth. I gaze at all the stars, constellations, galaxies, nebulae, and I imagine billions and billions of them...I become a human telescope scanning the infinite, zeroing in on specific sections of star clusters but unable to grasp it all in my mind. Still, I can encompass a great deal of what's out there, even if it's only a small fraction of the universe.

Think of all the energy, resources, light that's there. Think of the Solar System and imagine the untapped wealth and the undiscovered sources of energy. Whoever told us that we had an energy crisis had a very limited view of the universe.

Think of Earth. Buckminster Fuller demonstrated that there is enough abundance on the planet for everyone to be wealthy. Indeed, there is enough of everything, even now, for all life to flourish. There is a natural ecology which, when understood and respected, sees to it that life thrives. The problem is not lack of energy, resources, or money. The problem is lack of understanding, imagination, and correct action; the lack of loving relationships.

Think of all the money in the world. Begin with your home town. Think of all the money the people in your town possess. Now expand that to your region, and your country. Think of the national debt. Think of trillions and trillions of dollars. Write the number one with a dollar sign next to it. Then start adding zeroes. When you reach twelve zeroes, you've got a trillion. Keep going. Fifteen zeroes is a quadrillion. If you get to three hundred and three zeroes, you've got a centillion dollars. How easily you're back to one cent. It's the number one plus zeroes, unity plus circles. What does it all mean?

Think of outer space. Imagine it stretching out in every direction from you. If the universe is infinite, then space extends infinitely in every direction from you. Where does that place you? At the center, right? Then was Copernicus wrong? Hardly. But Copernicus was examining the nature of the dream not ultimate reality.

So there you are at the center. Think of others who live on the opposite side of the planet. They, too, have space stretching in every direction from them. So they are at the center of the universe, too. This would seem to indicate that the center of each of us is the same place. Dr. Deepak Chopra has illustrated this point in his books and lectures. Perhaps that's why we call it the "universe" which means "to turn towards oneness."

When you think of this vast universe, how do you think of

yourself in it? Are you little or big? Lonely or embraced? Poor or rich?

How can you be lonely when you are in the company of such abundance? How can you be poor when you are surrounded by such wealth? How can you be separate when you're at the center? And how can you be little when you can imagine so much? If your mind can stretch beyond the apparent limits of your physical reality, what does that say about who you are? Are you really this little, insignificant, impoverished speck of dust? Or are you a vastness of your consciousness which has the ability to extend beyond physical boundaries? Are you the centerpoint of the universe arising from the center of your individual being?

If we identify with our larger sense of self, then we can see that who we are is a unified consciousness which can both expand to include the whole and contract within diverse, individual, physical entities. But even when we contract within our smaller sense of selves, it is practical and profitable to remember that we remain interconnected with the abundance surrounding us.

If we were not already connected, we would be doomed to be separate. But we're not. When we meet someone, look into their eyes, and feel that instant connection—love, recognition, whatever, we are simply transcending our sleep state and waking up to the reality of quantum spirit. And by spirit, I don't mean something separate from matter. Rather, I refer to the less visible, but equally physical, aspect of life. It's no accident that when our eyes lock with those of another, we call it chemistry.

Let's apply this concept practically. If this vision of the universe and our location within it is valid, how could it, how would it affect the way we live? How would we feel within the dream if we could retain this vision in our minds? How would we feel, how would we act, how would we work, and how would we handle money?

I think we would relax more knowing that the universe

supports us. If we think that we are little and separate from a vast, disordered universe, we feel threatened and defensive. We hold onto what little we have. We mistrust support and resist receiving.

One of my favorite stories is of the man who went to Times Square in New York City and attempted to give away one-dollar bills. Most people thought he was just another nut and avoided him as if he was a panhandler. What would have been the response if he had tried to give away hundred-dollar bills? They would have locked him up, or put him in Bellevue for observation.

In our sleeping minds we think that the big universe is out to get us and we have to protect ourselves. This causes us to miss many good things in life. The root of our mistrust lies with the people who brought us into this cold, cruel world—the delivery team, who controlled, manipulated, and hurt us in the name of support.

In our larger identity, we can see beyond this scenario and envision the universe as quite intelligent, life-supporting, and generous. As Rev. Ike says it, "You can go to the ocean with a teaspoon or a bucket, the ocean doesn't care." We are the only ones who limit receiving. In the dream, we control our giving and receiving because we think that there's not enough for everyone. This causes tension and stress—even disease. Disease is the lack of ease. How can we have ease or the easy life when we deem life to be hard and harsh?

Given an abundant universe, we can see a wealth of benefits. We can cooperate and generate more for everyone instead of competing in a rat race. Moreover, we can make a living doing what we want rather than sacrificing our gifts and talents to merely survive. It's no accident that each of us has unique capabilities and interests. We were put here with a purpose, our part in the cosmic design. We are connected to the Intelligence running the show, and when we act consciously, we are in harmony with the universe and can produce wealth and satisfaction for ourselves and others.

This is the notion of "right livelihood." The word was originally livelode, Middle English for "course of life." Then it came to mean "the quality or state of being lively." Now it's a "means of support or subsistence." If we look at the concept of "right livelihood" in light of right course of life, then we can choose our careers based on what supports our overall direction in life. In other words, we can be whole instead of fragmented about our work. Moreover, we can be lively instead of half-dead at work. We can stop thinking that our survival is a function of something separate from the rest of our life. We can get clear on our personal missions in life and express that in our work.

Career comes from the Latin word carrus, meaning car, which then became carrarria, the road for vehicles. So, our careers are our vehicles to our life destinies, and the path we choose to take. We can drive a Mercedes or a Chevy, the road doesn't care.

We can expand our vision to apply our new values to our children—their birth, education, and upbringing. We can bring them into the world more gently and lovingly, preparing them for the good life and not a life that's tough and cruel. We can restructure our educational institutions to embrace this vision rather than drilling our children with useless information which has no value anywhere other than in the dream. We can allow our children to explore the abundant universe, their intimate connection to it, the value of harmonious relationships, and the importance of renewing the planet. We can teach love instead of fear. We can teach the new physics of healing rather than the old physics of pain.

We can create health care based on relaxation, ease, happiness, balance, and a knowledge of the whole as well as the parts. Rather than relying on medicine to fix sick people, we can have health centers based on living in tune with natural laws. We can focus on preventing disease by maintaining balance and harmony in mind, body, and spirit rather than repairing the body like a faulty machine when it springs a leak or blows a fuse. We can focus on wellness not illness.

We can review our institutions in the light of this vision and make practical revisions in the way we think, relate, and act. We can question age-old assumptions and traditions which are out of touch with reality. And we can restore the meaningful traditions that we've rendered obsolete in the name of progress. We can study certain pagan tribes, aborigines, and Native Americans, and learn how to reconnect with our planet. We can stop destroying our environment and debating the necessary steps to clean it up. If we're living in a mind-set that's sick or myopic, we're never going to attain true health or clarity. What's needed is a vision that can show us the alternative. If heaven on earth lies across the bridge, do we try to repair hell or simply cross the bridge?

Our vision can also examine wealth in a new light. If we see ourselves surrounded by and connected to an abundant universe, we no longer need to live in fear of insufficiency. We can trust, open up, and let ourselves receive more. We can accumulate more and know that it's just a drop in the bucket or a bucket in the ocean of endless wealth. We can save more, invest more, and use what we create to prosper the whole as well as ourselves as individuals. We can be more generous with our money, knowing there's always more and that it always comes back. We don't have to be greedy. Greed is trying to get more of what we believe there's never enough of. When we have the certainty of abundance, we can stop producing and consuming so much waste, junk, and useless products and open our eyes to our true needs. When our values are clear, we can discard everything valueless. We can individually and collectively devote ourselves to the creation of a world of true, unending wealth.

When we wake up, we will discover that we've been living in such a world all along.

◆ Chapter 4 ◆

Minding Your Own Business

Meanwhile, here we are in the dream, in the movie of our minds. Learning how the movie works can help us change our financial picture. Life imitates art. If we want to improve financially, we need to upgrade the movies of our minds. So, let's take a look at what I call "fi psy," financial psychology, and see how the metaphor of a movie can help us understand the mechanics of our financial projections.

How does a movie work? Basically, it's quite simple. We need a projector, a source of power, reels of film, and a screen. (Of course, we need to make the film first, but we'll get to that part later.) In our movies, our minds are the projectors; our films are the images, thoughts, and patterns of behavior we unconsciously project onto our lives; and the source of power is the light of God or the energy of the universe, whichever we prefer.

The way we manifest our financial experience or any experience is by channeling light through the thought forms in our minds onto the dream of life we call reality. For example, imagine you need $3000 to pay your monthly bills and when you look at your checkbook mid-month, you have only $1500 and have no idea where the rest will come from. You can see this in two ways. Either you can think that you don't have enough or you can think that you will have enough. Whichever thought you embrace will affect you emotionally as well as financially. Thought is creative. You spin the reel of your movies based on your perceptions of the half-empty or half-full checkbook and the result is your experience. The more we focus on emptiness, the emptier we feel. The more we focus on fullness, the more we'll continue to project that vision.

We can have mini-visions of endless wealth even within the dream. Or we can continue to project old scripts from old dreams upon present-time reality. Living in fear of not having enough or running out of what little we have are thoughts that actually produce chemical reactions in our bodies. Our brains send neuropeptides throughout our bodies and these "messenger molecules" cause us to feel what we think. We embody our thoughts. When we are feeling poor and hopeless about our financial future, we internalize these feelings. We become financially sluggish, lacking both the imagination and motivation to awaken from our self-imposed lethargy. What we think becomes what we feel becomes what we do becomes what we think. We then feel trapped in cycles of futility, and even this feeling is the by-product of the spirals of thoughts.

So, beware of the "poor me syndrome," which can not only depress us emotionally but cause lack and loss in all areas of our lives. I've seen too many people suffer from this syndrome who, even when they are financially healthy, project their poverty-consciousness onto other areas such as relationships. Their lovers suddenly leave them so that, subconsciously, they can justify their deep-seated need to feel sorry for themselves.

On the other hand, if we are financially optimistic, we spring into action. We believe that we are surrounded by wealth and that more money is always coming to us. We can begin to create success from this foundational thinking. When we're projecting the reels of prosperity consciousness, we feel excited not terrified about the future. Our paralysis turns into persistence. There is no scarcity of good money-making ideas. The only lack is lack of imagination, lack of vision. Unfortunately, many of us suffer from a wealth of such lack.

This might sound like good-old positive thinking, and there is certainly an element of it here. But there is one major difference. A positive thinker often ignores his subconscious and unconscious mind. Much of what we think is beneath the surface. The mind is like an iceberg; our conscious thoughts are just the tip of it. Most of the movie we create is buried in our unconscious minds, at least until we see it projected in our lives. It is, therefore, both practical and profitable to investigate the results, learn from them, and not cover them up with a blanket of denial or with superficial positive thinking. To transform our movie we must uproot the unconscious thoughts, images, and patterns that are contributing to our limited reality.

In other words, when you look at that $1500 in your checkbook, it might not be sufficient to imagine that you will generate the other $1500. Deep introspection may be required to release the emotional blocks lodged in your mind and body. It is only when we release the internal obstacles to wealth that we make room for the increase.

How do we do this? We've looked at how we project the film. Now we need to look at the way we made the movie we're showing. For instance, where did we get our ideas of scarcity from anyway?

It is important to acknowledge that we made the movie. We produced, directed, filmed, edited, and distributed it. And, of course, we starred in it. If we don't recognize the fact that we created it, we are powerless to change it. We're either pro-active or reactive, and there's not much in between. To acknowledge that we made the movie in the first place is not to say that we're failures. We may have successfully created a film about failure and successfully manifested it. But even failure is the key to future success, lessons to be learned which can enrich us.

We are responsible for our creations, but we are also innocent. The metaphysics of cause and effect does not imply moral culpability. We need to be careful when we use the word "responsibility." Blame, even self-blame, is always disempowering and counterproductive.

Once we realize that we made the film, we are liberated. We can now practice "mind management." Our minds are nobody's business but our own. Therefore, we owe it to ourselves to run it well. The better we are at running the business of our minds, the better our minds become at running the business of our lives.

You're the CEO in charge of a major production company. Begin by looking at your mind. Take stock of your mental assets. These include your healthy concepts of money and your positive money-making ideas as well as your high-quality thoughts about yourself, your relationships, support, trust, God and the universe. Then, observe your debits. These include your negative thoughts of lack, struggle, helplessness, and guilt.

Undergo financial self-analysis. Scrutinize, on paper, your mind as to why it insists on producing certain limiting results. Write at the top of the page, "The reasons I never have enough money are..." and allow your subconscious mind to spontaneously reveal the appropriate data. Many different types of thoughts might emerge. Separate them into categories: thoughts you learned from your parents, education, church, and primal thoughts—those you feel have been with you since birth.

The Sleeping Giant tried to teach the villagers to think big, but they became jealous, petty, vindictive. They were victims of their old, unconscious thoughts. We all are. For example, you may have learned at a very early age that you need a good education to be successful. Certainly, there are enough statistics to support this opinion. So you remained in school a long time and amassed degrees, only to feel disillusioned when you graduated and hit the marketplace. Reevaluate this line of thinking. Notice that the most highly educated people such as college professors, are not neccessarily the wealthiest and that there are many self-made millionaires with limited education.

You can change your mind. If you want a good business education, it is not necessary to attend the Harvard Business School. You don't need so-called experts to tell you what to think. All you need to learn is how to manage the business of your mind. Discard your debits, gather your assets. Vision and revision work.

Let's take another example. Perhaps you've always believed that you must struggle to survive. You might have struggled to be born, watched your parents struggle, observed the struggle in the world. You may have a rigid belief that the more you struggle, the wealthier you'll become. Reassess this point of view. Observe reality within the dream. Allow vision to enter your perception. Is it true that those who struggle the most accumulate the most wealth? Think of the poor who are struggling and not making it. No, struggling is not the source of wealth. Workaholics are the victims of a mental disease that harms their bodies and produces minimum financial remuneration.

Whether you're managing the business of your mind or the business of your life, don't confuse business with busy-ness. Often, we run around in circles pretending to be busy but really merely chasing our own tails. This is another example of the struggle pattern. We're expending energy, but it's not directed towards anything valuable. Or even worse, we see every problem as an emergency, crisis, life-or-death situation that must be solved yesterday. We forget to relax, take a break, and give ourselves the time and room for solutions to emerge. Much has been written about crisis management, and there certainly is great value in learning how to handle difficult situations calmly. But all too often, I observe people projecting crisis consciousness on what are ordinary problem-solving situations. Or they see a problem where there is none. If your movie is based on your addiction to struggle, creating false crises is the perfect script to follow.

We did a great deal of research when we constructed our movies. We didn't realize we were doing it at the time, but, as children, we learned from our parents, our teachers, and other role models. We imitated those we respected. After we learned our lessons, we buried the information in our subconscious minds. The way of the world became second nature to us. We recorded it with our inner cameras and imprinted it upon the film of our minds. Then, as we grew older, we took our seat in the theatre. We still do, unconsciously watching the movie of our lives go by, forgetting its origin, and mistaking it for truth.

Perhaps we suffer from financial prejudice. We prejudge the world of wealth around us, subjugating it to the tyranny of our limited thinking. Financial self-analysis can help us to see what we've done. It can also save us a great expense in business consultations. If you, for example, have inherited the belief that you are financially helpless, that the select few control everything, that you don't know enough about money, and that there's nothing you can do about it, you're suffering from a case of the financial blues. You're down and out in your own mind. You need help and you look outside yourself for it. Some people or companies spend a small fortune hiring business consultants to rescue them from their own feelings of inadequacy.

I'm not suggesting that we should not seek help when it's necessary. An outside opinion or a consultation from someone who can offer objective advice is invaluable. However, if we keep repeating a helplessness pattern, giving our power away to someone for the purpose of rescue, we are forgetting who is the real CEO. When we remember we're the boss, we take advice from everyone, but we are not weak and helpless in the process. We receive feedback from those around us without feeling threatened. We use the support we receive to clarify the business of our own minds. We know that the results are our best business consultants. We absorb this, process it, sort it all out, and make decisions for ourselves...decisions and revisions!

Never underestimate the power of reevaluation. When we subject ourselves to mental revisions, we wake up, little by little, to the reality of our vision. The commitment to our vision, the acknowledgement of our movies, and the courage to make revisions empower us as mind managers. So do our goals.

Goals are specific destinations along the path. They are neither our vision nor our purpose, both of which are timeless. Goals are mental points of focus in the dream. They exist in time and can be attained within the dream. Most of us were raised to be goal-oriented and to struggle to achieve our objectives. Many of us rebelled at this, realizing that the struggle was not worth the goal. Others succumbed to the struggle and did the best they could. Goals need not entail struggle. They can be simple signposts, oases on our journey.

The important thing to remember is that a goal, fixed in time and space, is limited. The value of a journey is never determined by whether or not a goal is reached. As travelers, sometimes, it is more important to take the scenic route than the direct route. Sometimes there are detours. Sometimes we change our minds about where we're going, based on new data and experiences along the way. Sometimes we go the long route to find future shortcuts. And there are times when we don't actually want what we think we want and learn that on the way.

We should never be slaves to our goals. However, we should not fear goals either. We should not avoid or deny them because we think it must involve struggle, or because we fear failure or success. Goals can be wonderful friends, allies, guiding forces in our lives. They can wake us up to our own potential, stretching us to discover new parts of ourselves. While they are no substitute for the pleasure of the journey, they can point us in a direction that harnesses our creative energy. We need to remember that we always have the power to revise our goals in the light of our vision.

All good movie-makers have their goals, and they change their minds countless times during the creative process. They get new ideas. They take risks. They examine their daily shoots at night and awaken the next morning with fresh and better ways of rendering their concepts.

All good businesspeople are organized. They have their goals, their plans, their strategies and their flowcharts. They also carefully keep track of results, frequently reevaluating and revising plans to attain their objectives.

All good mind managers know that their minds are their own business and that they are free to think what they choose. And they have the courage to change their minds when change is needed.

◆ *Chapter 5* ◆

In God We Trust

*I*always wondered why there were so many religious, political, and historical symbols on paper money. We've got pyramids on the United States dollar, royalty on the British pound, Greek gods on the drachma, national heroes on the French franc, pharaohs on the Egyptian pound, and even the skyline of Jerusalem on the Israeli schekel. Why all this misplaced hero-worship? Do we truly worship money as a false god? Are these symbols of our misplaced faith? Or do we place our heroes, gods, and warriors on our currency to represent our collective belief in lasting value?

When we think about it, the only value money has is the value we assign to it. Without our collective agreement, real money would become play money overnight. If suddenly no one was willing to pay more than a thousand dollars for a BMW 325I or more than one dollar for a pair of Nike sneakers, the ramifications throughout the world would be devastating. Everything, from the price of rice in China to the cost of coffee in Colombia would reflect this. If we woke up one morning and decided that the dollar, yen, mark, and pound had no value, so it would be.

We would set the global marketplace in total disarray. For even though it appears that inflation, deflation, recession, and depression are the results of either government regulations or mysterious economic laws and cycles, the truth is that we, the people, determine the inflated or deflated prices we pay for goods. It is our financial moodswings that ultimately determine the financial fluctuations in our local, national, and global economies.

Money has no value without our collective agreement and cooperation. If we calculated the actual value of a one-hundred dollar bill, we'd calculate the cost of the paper and the cost of the ink. All additional value is a leap of faith. Perhaps this is why the money-makers decided to place symbols of belief, trust, and tradition on our currency. They knew when they invented money that it would have to represent something it was not. And they carefully selected appropriate images to represent power, law, and order.

Originally, there was no money. I think it's important to remember that human beings survived for many thousands of years on this earth without money. They hunted, they farmed, they produced products and exchanged them at the marketplace, surviving very well. When we feel financial panic, thinking we cannot survive without more money, the memory of our ancient ancestors can serve us well.

One day someone had the bright idea that it would be far easier, faster, and lighter to exchange coins, then paper, instead of actual goods and services. Originally, these coins were worth their agreed-upon amounts. Paper money was backed by valuable minerals such as gold which could be used in exchange. But gradually, more paper money was manufactured than the gold that it represented, and the money game became more of a mystery.

We created the money game to lighten our load, then forgot its purpose and projected our emotions onto the game board. Now, we are just as exhausted dealing with paper and coins as we were previously bartering sacks of potatoes and herds of sheep.

Often we don't even carry cash. We simply punch different numbers on computers to move money. Yet as long as we are asleep in our collective financial dream, our psyches ignore how easy are contemporary money transactions.

Money has no value except in circulation. If you had stuffed a million dollars under your mattress and never spent a dollar of it, you'd be living in poverty. For money to have value we must keep it moving. Whether we spend it, save it, or invest it, we circulate it.

For example, when you deposit one hundred dollars in your savings account, you don't think that the teller puts your one hundred dollar bill in a drawer with your name on it and returns that money to you when you withdraw it, do you? Of course not. You may think of it as your money in the bank, but, in fact, it is now the bank's money to play with. The bank makes its profit by investing your money wisely and keeping the difference between the interest it receives and the interest it pays you. You are actually loaning the bank your money for its business.

How generous we are to keep our financial institutions afloat!

"In God We Trust," we print on the United States dollar. Who or what is this God whom we need to insure the value of our money? I think we once thought of God as an anthropomorphic presence in the heavens. Depending upon the intensity of our religious backgrounds, we may have matured from this egocentric projection of our own physical forms. Certainly, the more we investigate, the less evidence there is of an ancient man with a long, white beard sitting on his throne in a remote kingdom. But, equally clear, is that the more scientific evidence we gather, the more we reach the undeniable conclusion that there is an intelligent spiritual Presence governing the universe. Many of the world's greatest scientists—even Einstein were mystics at heart.

In every religious system, there are two aspects. The first, an intelligent Presence working behind the scenes. Call it God's will, the force, the universal law of physics, metaphysics, whatever.

This aspect is our sense that we do not live in a random universe, that what happens has a purpose, and that we are all a part of this purpose. We have glimpses of the Presence, moments of enlightenment, but within the dream we can never fully comprehend the big picture. All religions seem to agree on this point.

The second aspect, however, sparks tremendous disagreement, debate, and even devastation. This is the result of differing belief systems. Each religion has its own belief system, its laws and rules that define the will of the invisible Presence. One religion says that the truth is found in the Old Testament, another defends the New Testament, a third argues for the Koran, a fourth turns to the Vedas, while a fifth qoutes the Tibetan Book of the Dead. It is these varying interpretations of divine will that result in holy wars, each religion fighting to impose its belief system on the one it feels most threatened by. "Holy wars"—what a misnomer!

Holy terror is the new weapon of religious fanatics, terrorists who disrupt the global marketplace in the name of Allah, Jesus, Shiva, whomever. Fear is the precious commodity offered to us. And when we are confined to the dream of egonomics, we buy it. We know the consequences of an insane devotion to a belief system. The fact that a belief system is given in the name of God does not distinquish it from any other form of murder. We all have our little crusades and liberation fronts in our minds, but in our hearts we know that there is nothing holy about suicidal devotion. We can kill for Jesus or kill for Hitler, but we are still killers. And if we're making a killing on Wall Street, we may also have blood on our hands.

A spiritual Presence that is separate from any aspect of its creation is an incomplete spirit, lacking the universality we claim it represents. And a God that denies many in the name of a few is a separatist, which is contradictory to the principle of unity that governs the universe. Any deity who demands that we die for him or her is one not worth living for. If he or she asks us to kill someone, he or she is requesting that we destroy a vital part of ourselves. Thus, the projections of our ego's limitations onto spirit creates a distorted spirit, a spiritual egotism which can be the most dangerous of all forms of egotism.

So, let's forget about the limited thinking of little minds and return to the function of spiritual Presence. Let us assume that we are all entitled to our own beliefs, that each of our minds is nobody's business but our own, and that we can be secure enough within ourselves to be tolerant of diversity, if not celebrate it. In fact, let us return to our movie theatre and projector through which we run our reels of film. And let us think of the Presence as simply the light of God or the universal energy which empowers our projector to shed light on the images we feed it.

In God we trust. And God upholds our free will. Whatever we hold up to our mind's eye, we need God's electrical charge to transform the thought form into an experience. Obviously, this God is not an old man in the heavens. He, She, or It is an omnipresent force field in which the universe resides. This God exists in all space and time and beyond space and time which, after all, are just more sophisticated thought forms we project onto reality.

When we trust the unknown and unknowable intelligence governing the universe, we can trust life itself. When we have faith in the invisible, we can feel more secure with the visible. When we know that the source of life is energy, we can play the money game and enjoy it, knowing that our survival does not depend upon our success or failure. It's just a game.

Therefore, a deep, personal, spiritual connection enhances our prosperity consciousness by giving us the context in which to play with money. Without such a connection, we are caught in the world of egonomics, an urgent world filled with life-or-death decision making. With it, we know we can tap an abundant universe, an affirming force field and a loving intelligence for our own personal wealth and our commonwealth.

When we stop fearing God and start experiencing His love, the Sleeping Giant can awaken within all of us, guiding us back to the cave wherein our treasure lies. When we're trapped in our struggle to succeed, we don't easily see the value of stopping and renewing ourselves, physically, mentally, and spiritually. We can be so swept away by the dream that we forget how to pinch ourselves awake. We need a spiritual pinch now and then. The more we incorporate spiritual practices into our daily routine, the more time we spend in the field of endless wealth and the less time we waste in the dreamscape of scarcity.

Never underestimate the importance of your personal spiritual life. Discover ways to feel renewed and practice them daily. Whether you meditate, chant, read from holy books, listen to holy music, pray, attend service, do yoga, tai chi, rebirth—whatever works for you—do it regularly. It may seem to have nothing to do with your financial movie, but behind the scenes it does.

When you focus on the spirit, you expand the context. When you focus on your business objectives, you narrow your field of vision. Both are equally necessary in order to attain true and everlasting wealth.

Remember to start with the context. Begin each day with something relaxing and expansive. Not only will such beginnings give you more energy throughout the day, they will add to your creativity, your ease and your equilibrium in making important decisions.

When we're obsessed with narrow-minded objectives and neglect the spiritual context, we feel the stress. We pressure ourselves to solve problems and succeed, but we are blinded by our own lack of internal light, a light that only spirit can provide. The result is often frustration and failure.

We may even convince ourselves that we operate better under pressure. Then we subconsciously create urgent situations, place ourselves in the pressure cooker, and push full-steam ahead. Soon, however, we realize the debilitating ramifications of such behavior.

More and more people are practicing spiritual disciplines these days, but often the methods are misguided. Rather than relaxing into spiritual pleasure, some of us are too focused on the discipline aspect. We think that if only we labor at our spiritual connection, God will reward us with material benefits. Not only is this a transference of the struggle pattern to the pursuit of spirit, it is also spiritual bribery. We are projecting a parental authority onto God, trying to please Him, then expecting Him to give us our due. More egonomics and spiritual egotism.

We should feel joy, not struggle. We should celebrate our connection to spirit, not work hard to establish it. And we should express our gratitude through our practices, not our attempts to become worthy.

We are already worthy of God's love, and He already loves us. We were born into a loving, life-affirming, supportive universe. Money is an extension of that support. Life is a reward, a gift, a treasure more valuable than all the cash in the world. We already have the grand prize, the winning Lotto ticket, the pot of gold. We would not trade in our lives for all the money in the world, yet how often do we move from this sense of true personal wealth. We are so blinded by the quest that we forget the destination. Why do we want money? What is the reward we expect it to deliver? More material possessions? If so, what do we hope to feel? Happy? But we already have everything we need to be happy. And financial wealth, in and of itself, is never the key to happiness.

If happiness is the goal of wealth, if it is the true sunken treasure, let us open our hearts and rejoice now. Why wait to be happy? If we find happiness now, we can happily travel to our destination.

I have a statue of a Chinese god of prosperity. He is laughing, not because he's rich but because he's happy. He's in love with life.

So, let us rejoice with universal laughter. Let us reconnect with that primal spiritual devotion that so-called primitive tribes exhibit uninhibitedly. Let us pound on our drums, whirl like dervishes, and sit in circles of prayer.

I always liked the image of thousands of Chinese people practicing tai chi each morning. Wouldn't it be wonderful if each business acknowledged a spirit to start the day. We could sit in a circle and chant holy songs...or lay on our backs and breathe for twenty minutes...or meditate in silence...or start each day with a Quaker meeting. There would be no leader. We would wait for the spirit to move someone and he or she would stand up and express himself or herself freely.

The ego tells us that spiritual activity is a waste of time. But in our hearts, we know that when we look for the hidden treasure, we strike it rich.

When we trust our connection with spirit, we are truly financial giants, our cash flow merely a stream we observe.

• *Chapter 6* •

Beyond Egonomics

*I*n the dream a healthy ego is a wondrous thing. Then why is it we have such an ambivalent attitude towards it? The ego has certainly received an abundance of bad press in enlightened circles. We fear the proverbial "ego trip" as if such a journey, in and of itself, dooms us. Yet, without a healthy ego we would be lost in the sea of sleep, helpless to navigate ourselves towards a safe harbor.

The ego is absolutely necessary within the dream even though when we awaken we discover it had no lasting purpose.

When we are born and are overwhelmed by an avalanche of sensations, we experience tremendous fear. Perhaps we absorb this fear directly from our mothers, who, in giving birth, struggle in agony. When the umbilical cord is cut, we are separate and the fear becomes ours. According to Dr. Verney in *The Secret Life of the Unborn Child*, we quickly recover from the physical circumstances of our births. But the fear we have inherited stays lodged in our minds and bodies, dormant for the most part, only occasionally erupting in childhood nightmares or attacks of separation anxiety. Primarily, however, to return to our prenatal sense of safety, living in a universe that supports and loves us.

As we grow and learn about the nature of reality within the dream, we feed our knowledge with our primal fear, the memory from our birth. As we wean ourselves from our mother-identification and acquire appropriate boundaries, we achieve a greater and greater sense of separation and independence. We also perceive, from the information available to us, that what lies outside ourselves is not always supportive and friendly. We learn to mistrust, scrutinize, evaluate, and defend.

The ego is born and developed during this process of individuation. It is our internal ally in a world based on alliances and conflicts. It is our personal Pentagon, our Defense Department, safeguarding our separation and securing our survival. The ego is our declaration of independence, announcing to the world that we have the right to be free and, if necessary, will fight to protect that right. World, don't meddle with us.

We need to gain independence in order to evolve to the point of individual self-sufficiency. If we never transcend dependency and codependency, we will forever resent those we need and stay entangled in unfulfilling relationships. We want to be free, but we live in terror of letting go. We never learn that we can succeed on our own.

Economically, we need healthy egos to survive the rat race. When the ego is weak, we crumble under the weight of financial pressure. We think that the world is too powerful and we're too helpless. Then we project what is unresolved within us, judging the world to be wrong for its egotistical ways. Judgments are weapons of the internal Defense Department. What we judge we keep at a distance, forgetting that what we see is an extension of what we think of ourselves. A weak ego, therefore, keeps us asleep longer because it pushes our needed lessons further and further away.

A healthy ego embraces and attacks the world with vigor. It motivates us to dive into the sea of life and learn from experience. We become swimmers rather than observers from the shore. Financially, a healthy ego enables us to play the money game, to feel the joy of success and the pain of failure. We undergo the inner cycles of inflation and depression, expansion and recession. We may even learn that the only true recession is a receding prosperity consciousness.

The ego sells us tickets to a financial roller coaster ride, lifts us to its limits, drops us through the loops of economical cycles, and then abandons us because it can do no more. It gives us the dream of great glory within the big sleep, helps some to be a great success from time to time, and allows others to barely survive failure and play again another day. It sends some of us through the mill of dispossession, repossession, and emotional bankruptcy.

The ego also instructs us in practical matters. For example, it tells us to take a portion of what we earn and save it. Within the dream, saving is necessary because we never know what the future will bring. So we save for a rainy day. When we begin to awaken, we change our idea of saving. We open multiple savings accounts for different purposes—bills, travel, large purchases, taxes, investments. When we open these accounts, we attract more income. We're applying the principles of metaphysics to the dream. We're trying to get ahead of the game. The ego is still guiding our behavior, steering us towards the limits of its perceived reality.

The ego also teaches us to save, to budget, to live within our means. It advises us to manage our money cautiously, distributing our earnings within the walls of reason. It reminds us that we're living on a fixed income and warns us of the dangers of overspending.

The ego, however, tempts us to form an unholy relationship with money. Money becomes the object of our spiritual devotion. It's what we seek and what we fear, what we respect and what we obey. Money becomes the substitute for God. We place it on a pedestal, pray to it, and hope it will shed its grace upon us. If only enough money was showered upon us, we think, we would be in heaven.

When we perceive money as the source of our salvation, we will do almost anything to obtain it. Most of us are too honest to become thieves, but, nevertheless, we pay a personal price for money, often compromising our spiritual integrity doing what we think we need to do to survive. Money is the last refuge of the ego because it is the ego's ace in the hole when we want to escape its embrace. The ego whispers in our ear, "If you release me, you will lose the security I've given you. You can't survive a day without me." We know that money represents survival, and so we hang onto the ego as our financial manager.

God probably allows us to maintain an ego because He is generous and knows that the ego is a valuable teaching device to show us the dreamscape. However, when we make the ego our lover, we feel guilty because we know that we are rejecting spirit and selecting separation as a substitute reality. In choosing separation, we banish ourselves from the Garden. We exile ourselves from paradise and endless wealth, opting, instead, to reside in a world of pain, poverty, and spiritual emptiness. Thus we have a hungry heart.

So, while the ego has its assets, ultimately it does not deliver the goods of true wealth.

An egotist is one who loves the separate self more than the unified self. When we do this, we are not bad or evil. We have sinned only in the sense of the archer "missing the mark." We have missed the mark of correct unity consciousness and have, therefore, fallen from grace.

When we decide to leave God's kingdom we are in a state of guilt and, therefore we secretly fear punishment. We often don't feel guilty at this stage because guilt is not so much a feeling as a condition. When we're in this state, we fear God will attack us for rejecting His heaven. But God has no interest in punishing us.

We have already punished ourselves by choosing the dream of separation. God simply awaits our inevitable return. As *A Course in Miracles* tells us, God has no need to forgive us because He holds no grievances. He sees our guilt as being part of the dream and, therefore, unreal.

As for punishment, it is self-inflicted once we choose to explore the territory outside the Garden. Struggle, conflict, fear, anger, pain, disease, poverty, depression, helplessness, shame, abuse—given the landscape of our chosen dream, what further punishment could God possibly offer? Death? Would that be a punishment or a welcome relief?

The ego is the great dream-maker, the Cecil B. deMille of our epic guilt. Nevertheless, the ego is not our enemy as much as it is a friend and a teacher. As long as we stay in the company of the ego, we have a lifetime companion in this cold, miserable world. There are, however, places the ego cannot take us. It cannot lead us beyond its own boundaries of separation and paranoia. It cannot open the door to true love, happiness, health, or endless wealth. It is unable to provide us with spiritual well-being because it has a different purpose. We should not be disillusioned with the value the ego does offer, nor should we expect more than it promises. When we strike a deal with the ego, we are exchanging our vision of the commonwealth for survival of the financially fittest.

The ego always keeps its part of the deal.

When we reach that point where we've gone as far as the ego can take us and we're still not happy, not satisfied, and not fulfilled deep within, we are at the crossroads between the dream and the vision. We are stirring in our sleep but not yet awake. Often, at this point we feel despair. We've worked so hard, given our all, and feel empty inside. This hopelessness is spiritual bankruptcy, which is not the end of the day, rather, the darkest hour before the dawn. When we sink to the lowest point, we have the opportunity to realize how much we've spent spiritually for the gifts of the ego. The ego has done its job perfectly. It has taken us through the labyrinth of the dream. It has led us to the edge of the awakened state. It can do no more.

We have not wasted our time, though it may appear so. When we learn the lessons of the ego, we realize that there is nothing wasted in God's universe. It is perfect even within the dream.

Hopelessness is "less-hope-ness." It means that we have no hope that the ego can deliver the spiritual goods. We are absolutely correct in this realization. But what is hope? It's wishful thinking. It's thinking that our power lies outside ourselves and, if we're fortunate, power will smile upon us. When we give up all hope, we are ready to take the leap of faith. Faith is the deep emotional conviction that we are guided. Faith is our passion for the unknown, or invisible, our essential trust that when we take the great leap we will land back in the original Garden. It's the knowledge, the certainty, that our vision is not a dream but, rather, a glimpse into reality. When we accept our hopelessness and take the leap of faith, our eyes open to the long-forgotten truth. At this point, we lose our previous ground of being, we spin in midair, and we become the financial giants we were born to be.

High self-esteem is different from a healthy ego. When our self-worth is developed, we are humbled to be a part of God's magnificent universe. We know that we are only a part of the majesty, yet we are unique and extraordinary. We celebrate the gifts that we have been given and our invaluable aspect of creation, but we never forget that we are nothing without the Creator supporting us. Such self-esteem is the true foundation for endless wealth. We can only attain this state of magnitude when we awaken to the whole and its miraculous design.

We can transcend these laws of egonomics. May we be grateful for their lessons and laugh at them a little:

THE LAWS OF EGONOMICS

I.   The universe is cold, cruel, and chaotic.

II. Life is a precious accident which could end at any moment.

III. Rely on your separate self and no one else.

IV. Only the financially fit survive.

V.   There is not enough for everyone.

VI. You can pity the poor, but you can't indulge your conscience and hope to succeed.

VII. You can lose everything you have in one moment.

VIII. You have limited time so don't waste it.

IX. Every problem is a crisis so it's urgent that you find immediate solutions.

X.   If you want to be successful, you must be ruthless.

XI. Other people are useful if you use them to your advantage.

XII. Make yourself indispensable to others.

XIII. Since money comes from others, be kind but don't fool yourself.

XIV. There's a sucker born every minute.

XV. Acquire as much as you can as fast as you can.

XVI. To acquire wealth, find out what people think they need and convince them that you have it.

XVII. Since everyone is afraid, appeal to people's fears of not having what you have to offer.

XVIII. Know your competition. Steal their good ideas whenever possible.

XIX. Inflate your asking price, then appear generous when you settle for less.

XX. Avoid spending money on yourself. Avoid generosity.

XXI. Since money is scarce, hoard what you get. Hide it, too.

XXII. Avoid paying taxes. Investigate Swiss banks and those in the Cayman Islands.

XXIII. During hard times, circle the wagons.

XXIV. Anticipate the worst possible financial scenario.

XXV. Never tell anyone the truth about money.

XXVI. Find an accountant who has few scruples.

XXVII. Get a good lawyer.

XXVIII. Always remember this: If you worship your ego, your ego will give you everything you want.

Obey these laws until you feel the need to become an outlaw. And rest assured, so long as you embrace egonomics, the Sleeping Giant will not bother you.

• *Chapter 7* •

Who's the Boss?

O ne of the seminars I offer is called "Rejuvenate Your
Career." I begin by telling my audience that everyone is
self-employed, whereupon there is usually a collective
restless stir in response. Certainly, we don't usually think of ourselves as permanently self-employed. More often, we think that
some of us work for ourselves and some work for others. Obviously, I am referring to a different concept of self-employment.

We are all independent contractors. Whether we are one-
person operations, hire employees, or hire ourselves out to other
companies, we are, essentially, in business for ourselves. We all
have our individual business purposes, skills, training and experience. If we realize that we work for ourselves, we are empowered to prosper further. Even if we are employed by others, it is
advantageous to consider ourselves independent contractors on
temporary assignment.

I often recommend to those searching for employment that
they list all the qualities of their ideal jobs. I ask them to be very
specific and to include the nature of work, the work environment, the quality of office relationships, the hours, the pay, vaca-

tion time, health insurance, pension—the entire gamut. I then suggest that they interview companies to see which ones they might want to hire. To the ordinary mind, asleep in the dream, such a suggestion turns their projection of the business world topsy-turvy.

Yet isn't it true that you choose your job? If you think otherwise, if you wait to be chosen, if you run the movie of "there's a scarcity of jobs out there for me and I'll be lucky if anyone hires me," you are rendering yourself powerless in the marketplace. You are imposing your worst case scenario on your vision of reality.

When we go to the supermarket, we don't buy food that chooses us. We select what we want. When we look for new homes, we don't go with the hope of finding houses that choose us. We look for environments that feel comfortable to us. And when we desire loving relationships, we look for one that will give us what we want. At least, I hope we do.

Some people, I realize, wait to be chosen before they choose anything. These are the helpless ones, needing others to decide for them, hoping they will be taken care of by whatever or whoever selects them. When it comes to job opportunities, I think more people are caught in this helpless mode than in any other area of life. Many of us want to fall in love, be oblivious, and have someone take care of us. But even more of us want to fall into a decent job, do something routine we can handle, and receive a regular paycheck. There's nothing wrong with this. It's a natural part of the dream. But we all need a wake-up call if we want to attain true wealth.

If we think of ourselves as self-employed, we immediately uplift ourselves from dependent and codependent relationships with our business associates. If we select a job that does not satisfy us, we can fire our employer and seek a better place to offer our services or products. We are independent contractors, our personal businesses larger than any one job. Furthermore, we avoid the emotionally charged notion of unemployment when we are between jobs. We are no longer unemployed but, instead, self-employed and surveying the marketplace, a far more uplifting concept.

I always suggest to my clients and students that they open personal business accounts. This is a way of cementing the concept of self-employment. Channel all your money through your personal business account. Then deposit what you want in your personal checking account. You might even want to invent a powerful name for your personal business account, such as "Wealthy William Unlimited" or "Prosperous Paul Enterprises."

Thinking of yourself as self-employed is a great boost to your self-esteem. You begin to tap the entrepreneurial spirit that may by lying dormant within you. Your creative imagination awakens, and you begin to think of new ways of attracting wealth and increasing the wealth you already possess. If you are temporarily employed at a business, you might start a secondary business you can nurture during your spare time. Someday one of these secondary businesses might become your primary source of wealth.

John Grisham, author of *The Firm,* was a lawyer for many years. One day he witnessed a horrible trial which triggered the impulse to begin the novel, *A Time to Kill.* Continuing his legal career, he'd write in his spare time, at least one page each day for a year. Eventually, he completed the novel, and, after many futile efforts, got it published. It was not a great success but it led to his second novel *The Firm* which became a best-seller. I've heard many stories like this and not only about writers.

Perhaps I've convinced you that it can be profitable to think of yourself as self-employed. The next step is to remember who is the self that is employing you. Is it your ego-self or your God-self? I don't think you want to go to work for your ego. The pay is bad, the hours are long, and there are little or no fringe benefits. Besides, the ego is a tyrannical boss, demanding your total obedience to its shallow-minded view of the universe, life, relationships, work and money. Your God-self, on the other hand, is your ideal employer. It gives you the freedom in decision-making. It stresses love over fear. It wants you to relax, enjoy your career, and be amply rewarded for your creative efforts.

If you're working for your ego, you've joined the endless rat race. If your God-self is in charge, you're embracing a vision of endless wealth.

When you manage the business of your mind, which is the first step in being successfully self-employed, it is important that you distinguish between the voice of your ego-mind and the voice of your God-mind. The former will be very tense, loud, dictatorial, or seductive; the latter will be gentle, powerful, and ring true. Learning to discriminate is the choice between following the orders of your inner tyrant and trusting your intuition. One leads you down the path of diminishing returns while the other guides you to the commonwealth you seek.

The next step in being successfully self-employed is to know your purpose in life, and then your business purpose. Your purpose is not the same as your goals. Your purpose is your essential reason for being. Most of us have simple purposes, such as "to create," "to play," "to express myself," "to love nature," or "to communicate clearly." Sometimes your purpose seems so deceptively simple you can't believe it's true. Yet whenever you act purposefully, you are happy, and whenever you veer off purpose, you are not. At these times, you should focus on that which would immediately bring you back on track, such as spiritual practices, loving relationships, and ten favorite pleasures, a list of which I suggest you keep handy.

Our business purpose is our spiritual purpose applied to money. For example, my business purpose is "to create wealth through self-expression." Whether I'm leading a seminar, writing a book, or consulting with a client, this business purpose is my throughline, my reason for doing what I'm doing. A business purpose might be "to attain wealth by promoting clear communication," or "to become financially independent by creating beauty," or "to flourish financially by nurturing the natural environment." Take a few minutes to allow your intuition to guide you to your spiritual and business purposes. When you do this, don't be too intellectual. Don't struggle for the right answer. Just allow the quiet voice to emerge with the words you need to hear.

Now you can move on to your mission, which Steven Covey discusses so wonderfully in his book, *The Seven Habits of Highly Effective People.* Your mission statement can be a great asset to your personal business. This is your statement to yourself and to the world, clearly identifying your values, priorities, principles, and concerns. In a way, it's your integrity checklist. It's also separating your purpose into component parts. Your mission statement is your declaration of independence, your constitution, your state-of-the-union address. You should write a personal mission statement and then a business mission statement.

The above suggestions comprise the preliminary work required for creating your own business. If you never work for yourself in the traditional sense, you will gain great value and insight by becoming clear on your purpose and mission. And if you choose to work for yourself, you will have a healthy spiritual and mental context from which to make decisions.

Once you have your purpose and mission defined, you can progress to your goals, your business plan, and your strategy for success. You can organize your time so that you are moving forward each day toward accomplishing your objectives, doing the necessary tasks and taking the necessary steps, one by one. Wise businesspeople think big, develop the spiritual context, and then divide their time between the vision and the practicalities that matter so much. They are not afraid of or bored by routine because they know that in repetition lies repeated success. "Business as usual" is the motto for business wealth.

When we're stuck in the dream, however, we are constantly

wasting our time either managing crises, daydreaming, or diverting distractions. We are unfocused and therefore, at the mercy of more persistent forces.

As self-employed people, we also need to learn to trust others. It's one thing to realize that we are the source of wealth. It's another thing entirely to realize that we create wealth only by receiving from others. If we don't have a sense of a supportive universe, then we will never trust the people who want to support us. We will think that we must accomplish everything ourselves. We will never grow in business if we don't learn to trust, delegate, and allow others to work for and with us. To expand financially is to stretch our relationships.

We also need to avoid the temptation to work too much. Becoming a workaholic is a major danger for the self-employed. When we love what we're doing and we are only accountable to ourselves, we can easily forget about the rest of our life. In traditional business, people take vacations to recover from the stress of work. The understanding is: life is a struggle, work is tough, and people need a few weeks to recover their energy. When we're not initially involved in the struggle mentality, we might think that we're enjoying our work so much that we don't need a vacation. We might think that work is a never-ending joy ride. So we cruise along on sheer excitement and adrenalin and then, one day, wake up and can't get out of bed. We're burned out.

When you are self-employed, it is critical that you organize your time wisely. You must be a benevolent boss to yourself. Working four days a week and three weeks a month might support your business more in the long run than going full-steam ahead without any time off.

I am about to begin a nine-month stretch of very intense work. In the past, I might have planned to take a vacation at the end of this period. Now I am more aware. I am taking one month off before I start, and then two months off when I complete it. Of course, I am also writing this book. But I'm not on any schedule.

My wife and I have decided not to structure plans this month. We wake up each morning and decide what we want to do. Or we don't decide anything and just breeze through a spontaneous, disorganized, pleasureful day.

If your goal is financial independence, then you must prepare yourself in the process. For days, weeks, and months, you should act as though you have already achieved it. Save money for these rehearsals for wealth. They may be your most intelligent investments.

When you're self-employed, you are free, but only insofar as you claim that freedom. What good is your freedom if you never seize it and use it to fulfill your deepest desires? What is the victory in working for yourself if you're still a slave to the unconscious patterns of your ego?

You can be a sleeping giant whether you work for yourself or are employed by others. And when you awaken from the dream and open your eyes, you discover that you were the boss in either case. You made the choices; you suffered the consequences; you reaped the rewards. You made your deals based either on your ideals or what you perceived as reality.

So, do yourself the greatest favor. Fire your ego, hire your spirit, and master the art of self-employment.

♦ *Chapter 8* ♦

Whistle
While You Work

The more we discover the correct course of life for ourselves, the more we are able to participate in the correct course of life for the planet. Since the earth is a family business, the more each of us practices the right livelihood, the more the global village flourishes in health, wealth, and well-being.

When I was in high school and college, I envied those who knew what they wanted to do when they grew up. Even more, I wished I had been born someone like Mozart, whose fingers reached for piano keys almost as soon as he could walk. My lot in life seemed so much more complicated. I had so many interests and a variety of talents, and I wanted to experiment in many different directions. It seemed to take me forever to decide on one career, and when I finally did, it was the last thing I would have anticipated doing. My mother always said I'd be a late bloomer, perhaps because I was born to my parents late in their childbearing years.

Looking back at the course of my life, I wouldn't change anything, and now I see a continuous training, preparation, and apprenticeship for my life's work of healing relationships. But then, asleep in the wilderness of my mind, I was groping for direction. At times it seemed like I'd never be able to combine all the things I loved to do into one career, let alone be successful in the process.

From India we learn the ancient concept of karma yoga, which is the belief that work, approached properly, can be a means of cleansing the soul. When I first studied yoga, I attended a series of seven-day retreats with the guru, Swami Satchidananda. They were silent retreats held in the beautiful Santa Cruz mountains, and consisted of good, healthy living—simple food, yoga exercise, chanting, and karma yoga.

My first assignment was to clean the toilet bowls. No wonder my initial impression of karma yoga was that it was "shit work." At first I resented my job, considering it the worst possible luck, but, as I persisted, my attitude improved. I realized that there were two ways I could approach my work. I could either resent it as unimportant and disgusting and do a quick, sloppy job to get it done; or I could see it as an opportunity to do something very simple very well, applying my best effort, full attention, and desire for perfection. My toilet bowls could either be dirty work or works of art; it was entirely up to me.

In a sense, I was actually doing dirty work glorified by the concept of releasing karma. But the more I made it a moving meditation, sinking into a state of absolute whiteness, the more I shined the porcelain bowls perfectly clean and the more I enjoyed it. The more I focused on the task and nothing else, applying creative strokes to my efforts, the more pride I took in my work and, who knows, the more karma I may have actually dissolved.

I began to see karma yoga as the release of resentment through work. Resentment is what keeps the wheel of guilt and punishment spinning. When I could experience gratitude or, at least, a spirit of forgiveness, I could see that this job was as good as any other. What seems to matter most is not the prestige of the job as much as the quality we bring to it. Of course, I didn't wake up to a pile of wealth cleaning those toilets, but I did awaken to the value of facing the tasks life offers us with a cheerful disposition. I believe that this lesson has contributed to my success.

My next karma yoga assignment was to cleaning windows. This was a perfect assignment for me because, at the time, I was trying to heal my eyesight. I had worn glasses for many years and wanted to be free of them. Once again, I quickly noticed my two choices: to do this menial labor haphazardly, unconsciously, and begrudgingly; or meticulously, consciously, and joyfully. I could focus on either the dirt and smudges on the window or the perfectly clear view. A voice in my mind said, "Clean the window until you can't see it any more." And so I did, scrubbing away every minuscule smear until the glass was transparent and all that I could see was the green grass, towering trees, golden hills, and blue skies beyond.

The window was like the lens of a camera or the "I" of the see-er. When I could dissolve the medium of seeing, I felt totally connected to the seen. Within a few weeks of my karma yoga, my eyes improved so much that I could drive at night and watch a movie from the rear of the theatre without my glasses.

Several years later, Mallie and I were facilitating an LRT (Loving Relationships Training) in Los Angeles. Sondra Ray, author of the training, offered to be Mallie's personal assistant for the weekend. At first, we were shocked. Not only was Sondra the boss; she was also a formidable lady—six feet tall, expensively dressed, and one accustomed to receiving care and service. The thought of her serving Mallie seemed demeaning. But, the more we thought about it, the more sense it made from every point of view. Mallie accepted her generous offer and Sondra served Mallie that weekend with all the gusto, joy, and desire for absolute perfection that she exhibits when leading a group. She ironed Mallie's clothes so they were completely wrinkle-free, arranged them neatly, in order, in the closet, even having the shoes line up in appropriate sequence. To her there was no difference between being on the front stage or behind the scenes. Her commitment to excellence was the same. Sondra was doing her job as perfectly as possible. She was just being herself.

Mallie loves to do the laundry. In fact, she loves to tend to the house, inside and out, whether it's tidying up, feeding the birds, or watering the garden. She thrives on nurturing her environment. When we began to travel around the world for our work, she learned to delegate many jobs, but she never gave up the karma yoga of home management. She says it grounds her. Sometimes, when we return after a long European tour, Mallie will walk into the house, weary-eyed, and reach with relish for the laundry. I'll try to discourage her. I'll remind her that she doesn't have to do it, we could hire someone, or I would do it myself. Mallie will inevitably strike her famous pose, rolling up her sleeves and resting her hand on her hips. She'll smile, take a breath, and refresh my memory. She'll tell me how much she enjoys doing the laundry, how it centers her after working with people's energy, and how it connects her to the rhythm of home. Then she'll proceed to wash and dry loads of clothes, sheets, pillowcases, and towels, neatly folding them in perfect piles she'll carry to their perfect places in the house. I have learned to appreciate Mallie's karma yoga as a ritual and a ceremony that is meaningful to her.

Our egos would lead us to believe that there are important jobs and unimportant jobs, and that if we want to be important people, we should concern ourselves only with important jobs and major events, endeavors that bring fame and fortune. We should, therefore, avoid the unimportant jobs but if it is absolutely necessary, then do them quickly and without regard for detail or quality. After all, they're not important.

But the truth is that when it comes to the life of an individual or the life of a business, success is always comprised of thousands of little details, chores, and tasks which alone seem unimportant but when added together can amount to huge accomplishments. Our attitude toward the little things will ultimately affect the grand scheme of our lives more than we realize. We cannot construct a magnificent cathedral unless we take pride in laying each stone.

When I was in drama school, I was taught that there were no small roles, only small actors. In other words, no matter how minor our characters seem to be, it is our job to exhibit a complete personality. Even a walk-on part has a full life for an actor with presence.

Never underestimate the richness of a small task.

We like to think that we have jobs which produce income which, in turn, allow us to live the way we choose. We want to separate our livelihoods from the rest of the course of our lives. In one sense, this might seem healthy since we don't want to be workaholics. However, the part of our minds that insists on separating work from play, money from love, weekdays from weekends, and workdays from holidays often leaves us unnecessarily fragmented.

Life is, in essence, one inseparable course of activity. Whatever life presents to us as the next task to be accomplished, we can be grateful for the opportunity or resentful for the obligation, depending upon the point of view we choose. If we resist what needs doing, we struggle. We don't want to be there. Our minds are elsewhere. We don't do a good job...and we become sloppy workers.

Recently, there was a backlash when a Japanese business magnum suggested that the problem with the American economy was that American workers did not do quality work. Granted, it was an undiplomatic thing to say, but is it true? And elsewhere? Are we thinking about other things when we could be applying ourselves more fully? Are we too distracted? Are we daydreaming? Sleepwalking? Are we questioning our livelihoods, wanting to be somewhere else doing something else and, therefore, missing the opportunity for growing, learning, and feeling the pride and satisfaction of a job well done?

All too often we regard work as a necessary burden of life rather than a path towards self-realization. If we don't love our work, we should consider a more spiritually rewarding alternative. But, in the meantime, we should become masters of what we do.

Have we lost a service mentality as well? Are we so afraid of servitude, exploitation, and abuse that we reject the attitude necessary for serving others well? Are we equating humility with humiliation we've felt in the past? Are we rebelling from and sabotaging service, not realizing it is at our own expense?

An enlightened service mentality is the attitude of providing support for others as a means of self-development. Obviously, the more support we generate for others, the more support each of us receives. When we learn to serve, we are learning how to give freely, without obligation. This is a core lesson in love, a lesson which will improve all our relationships. To master the receiving part of giving and the giving part of receiving, we must practice loving support and service, at work and at home.

However, we are obsessed with receiving love rather than giving it. Again, the "what's in it for me" attitude immediately eliminates the value we could receive. Too often, we give begrudgingly of ourselves; we do the minimum, give so little to get so much, and think we're being clever. Actually we're cheating ourselves. If we continue withholding ourselves at work, we limit true success and wealth. And the habit of withholding will come home with us, undermining our most intimate, personal, loving relationships.

Yes, we need to return to taking pride in our work. Do what you love whenever possible. However, when something else presents itself that needs doing, be the one to do it...and do it well. Love what you do, how you do it and for whom you do it.

When you take such pride in your work, you see your life as a continuum of undivided activity, as right livelihood. You naturally value an honest day's work, not cutting corners. Integrity becomes a personal value, not something you feign to gain approval. You realize that with integrity, you live a more integrated life, and that experience of wholeness is wealth that money can never buy.

Recently, we had a very unpleasant experience regarding our house in Greece. A Greek friend of ours offered to redo our simple home, promising to make it the most spectacular dwelling in our village. He was a famous fashion designer, film costumer, artist, and architect, and was extremely wealthy. We trusted him, gave him a good deal of money, and drew up a list of what he would do for us. It was a disaster. He hired cheap, incompetent labor; did a sloppy and unprofessional job; painted our tiled floors toothpaste blue; and failed to deliver many of the goods he had promised. All in all, it was a minor Greek tragedy.

We learned from this to take charge ourselves and proceed in a different way. We then interviewed local people with a reputation for excellence, honesty, and reliability. We finally hired a simple man, a stone-worker who was in business with his son and brother-in-law. He gave us a fair price, looked us in the eye, and assured us that we would not be disappointed. We could see the pride he had in his family business and we compared his obvious integrity to the flamboyant dishonesty of his predecessor. We shook hands. I could almost feel his conviction in the strong but warm clasp of his hand.

So, we should whistle while we work, work while we whistle, and know that karma yoga is not dirty work but, rather, both a training in excellence and a way to approach the course of our lives. And don't worry, we won't become financial dwarfs if we make work a moving meditation. On the contrary, the sleeping giant within will be awakened!

Chapter 9

Trust the Heart of the Deal

*I*remember when one of my students stood up in a crowded seminar room and called me "a snake oil salesman." Everyone laughed, myself included. In the past, I would have been offended, but, by that time, my opinions of both salesmen and snake oil had changed considerably. Also, I was secure enough to have a healthy sense of humor about the way I was perceived.

It is unfortunate that so many of us have such a strong aversion to sales as a profession. We mistrust salespeople almost as much as politicians. Yet selling is the core of business, and without it there would be no exchange of goods or services. Some of us flatter ourselves by thinking that our careers have nothing to do with selling. But we all sell ourselves along the way, whether we're at a job interview, or trying to generate clients, or wanting our students to buy what we're teaching. We all have our shingles out there somewhere.

Our attitudes towards sales will help to us determine our success or failure in the marketplace. If we think that selling is an unethical profession, we will withhold what we have to offer. We might withdraw our energy and resent the person buying from us. Why won't he or she buy from us without our having to sell? If images of used-car salesmen, hucksters, and hustlers cow us, we may crawl into our holes instead of facing the light of normal commerce.

I always enjoy visiting marketplaces in foreign countries, especially in the so-called "third world." I remember times in Mexico, Egypt, Israel, or Bali when the energy, excitement, and enthusiasm of the market was a major highlight of my journey. Wall Street has that same energy. It's just another marketplace, only with numbers and ticker tape instead of actual commodities.

Once, in Jerusalem, I saw silver jewelry that I wanted to purchase for my family. The salesman was immediately interested, sensing my vulnerability. I held three or four items in my hands —necklaces and bracelets—and asked the price of each. He then offered me a "special deal" for the entire lot. When he told me the price, I laughed. Then he lowered the price and I chuckled. Finally, he gave me the bottom-line price, whereupon I rejected his offer, thanked him, and walked down the street. He followed me. I turned the corner, but he pursued me, continuing to lower his price as I said nothing. Finally, he mentioned a price I was willing to pay, so I turned around, smiled, and nodded. We walked back to the shop together, his arm around mine, both as happy as could be. We were friends, brought together by the joy of negotiation.

If we enjoy the game, we are winning when we play. And if we learn how to play the game so that everyone wins, every purchase or sale can enrich the commonwealth.

Selling is giving and receiving. The heart of business is an act of love, and, as with any act of love, it can be manipulative and unfair or liberating and just. Since you are in charge of the deal, whether you are buying or selling, you are the one who determines the outcome. Let's look at it as salespeople.

First you need an item or service to offer. If you choose

something that you don't value or enjoy yourself, you have compromised your integrity at the starting gate. Why would you want to share something which you have not gained value from? For money? That's a poor reason. When you betray yourself by selling what you yourself are not sold on, you don't deserve to prosper. Besides, it's far easier to sell what you love because your customers can feel your genuine enthusiasm. Part of what they are purchasing is your excitement. They want to feel good, too. So, when you share your joy and aliveness, you are the ultimate salesperson.

Of course, you never want to force your item on your customer. If they do not want what you are offering, you must be willing to take no for an answer and let go of the sale. It is part of your desire that everyone wins. How do you win when you don't make a sale? You win because your integrity makes you a more worthwhile person.

Even the best baseball players fail to get a hit more than they succeed. If you bat 300, that means you don't succeed seven out of ten times. You are considered a great batter if you fail more than you succeed. And a good batter learns something every time he or she is at the plate which can help him or her the next time. A good salesperson is similar. You can calculate your batting average. If you know you're a 300-hitter, then you know you have to approach ten people in order to make three deals.

Never take your rejections personally. We are not being rejected if our products or services are unwanted by a particular customer. Selling can be such a wonderful process of developing self-esteem. We all have a rejection quota in life. When we've been rejected enough times, we stop rejecting ourselves and then others say yes more often. When we can accept our failures at the marketplace, we're well on the way to accepting rejection in all our relationships. We can love ourselves even when others say no. We're simply learning and successfully processing our own rejection quota.

Our self-esteem is our self-worth, which determines how much others value us. The more valuable we are to ourselves, the more we create value in the marketplace. It's important to remember who we really are. We can't put a price tag on how much we're worth. We are priceless works of art. If people reject what we're offering, it's their loss...or a transaction not meant to be.

If we remember the spiritual source of our self-worth, we will release much of our performance anxiety. We can relax into the certain knowledge of our lasting value and avoid bringing an urgent do-or-die mentality to our work. We can breathe easily. We can laugh. We can play with the energy and have fun.

I often suggest to my students that they find a one-dollar item they value and keep selling it until they reach their sales goal, be it a hundred dollars or a thousand dollars. If we start with something simple and inexpensive, we can avoid spending a fortune to create a business. Think of the man who invented post-its. He's a millionaire now. Even if we don't intend to make sales our career, mastering the game will contribute to our value in the marketplace.

What happens when your customer wants what we're offering? Then your job becomes the art of negotiating. Everything is negotiable. I once proved this to myself by negotiating such items as Baskin-Robbins ice cream cones, my tax returns, and even my telephone bill. Of course, sometimes you want to negotiate and the person, refuses, wanting a flat fee. Okay. Then you say no if the price is too high. End of deal. Still, everyone wins.

You should have an asking price and a bottom-line price when you are selling. Your asking price includes your desired profit. Your bottom line includes your minimum acceptable profit. If someone wants what you're offering, tell him your asking price first, then, if necessary, negotiate until you reach the price that is mutually acceptable. You can enjoy negotiating if you remember that it's a game, your survival or self-esteem is not based on any one transaction, you can take no for an answer, and you deserve to receive compensation for sharing your excitement about something you genuinely value.

We should learn to have gratitude and appreciation for those who serve us by selling to us. Think of all the valuable and beautiful possessions you've owned in your life. Where would we be without the people who were willing to sell these items? If no one sold us an airline ticket, we could not fly to Barbados and lie on the beach. If no one sold us a car, we'd be without one. And if no one sold us the food we eat, the house we live in, and the clothes we wear, we'd suffer the consequences. You might want to make a list the items you value and try to remember the individuals who sold them to you. Then, close your eyes and say, "Thank you very much." When you write a check to pay for a product or a service, you might also want to put a few words of gratitude on the check.

Regarding all those unscrupulous salespeople you've had to deal with, I suggest you forgive them and know that they have compromised themselves more than they have short-changed us. Don't worry. They will learn their necessary lessons. And even these people have been valuable in our lives. They have taught us how not to sell.

In a way, we were all born salespeople. When we came out of the womb, our parents took one look at us and agreed to spend a small fortune raising us. If it wasn't in our nature to attract support for the value we bring into the world, we would never be as well provided for as most of us are.

It is our innocence that allows us to play the money game and win. As children we play Monopoly, buying and selling Boardwalk and Park Place, railroads and hotels. We know that it's just a game. We use play money and miniature buildings, moving our pieces around the board. The only reason the game works is that we agree to its rules and enjoy playing. It can be the same as adults. The money is still paper. There are still rules. We agree to play by them. And there is an opportunity to share excitement while playing.

Buying and selling can be a loving game, too. We must learn to bring love to our buying and selling if we hope to share the true commonwealth of our vision. When we complete a transaction, we shake hands, a symbol of unity and friendship. It is in the global marketplace that salvation is won or lost.

The choice is always ours.

I recommend that we practice an enlightened way of keeping score when we are selling. Normally, we keep score as we go and our emotional well-being is determined by our daily successes or failures. This is nerve-racking. We ride the roller coaster of temporary fluctuations. A better way, in my opinion, is to keep the big picture in mind. We may experience periodic slumps each year, as well as brief hot streaks. We should wait until the end of the year before evaluating our performances. We might experience a year or two long slump. But possibly, after five years, when we look back at our batting average, we're 300-hitters after all.

I remember the best salesman I ever met. My wife and I were on holiday in Greece and visited an island called Mykonos. It was love at first sight. We only had a week there, but we wanted to stay forever. The light, the sea, the beaches, the food, the shops, the people—it seemed like heaven on earth. We had recently sold a coop in New York. We had bought it years before at the insider's price of ten thousand dollars and sold it for a hundred and ten thousand. Now, that was a profit. We decided to buy a house in Mykonos. We felt it was a way to guarantee our return trip. We searched the island and found an area we particularly liked. The salesman seemed to appear out of thin air. His name was David, I think. He hardly spoke. We walked with him, looked at the flowers, the private beach on the beautiful blue Aegean Sea, the Olympic-size swimming pool, the traditional Mykonian houses, none larger than two stories, and we bought one that day.

Did David sell us our place in the sun? Or did we sell it to ourselves in his presence. His brilliance as a salesman was in not interfering with our process of purchasing something we obviously desired. In all the years we have returned to our Mykonian home, we have never seen this man again. He disappeared from our lives as instantaneously as he appeared. Was he even real? Was he a creation of our collective will? Or did the universe bring him to us at the right time and place to experience one perfect moment of love and money in the marketplace.

Or was he the world's greatest snake oil salesman?

• *Chapter 10* •

Financial Boundaries

T here is a tendency today to go overboard making movies. In the dream, when we awaken to the fact that we are the dreamer, we often feel so liberated that we think we can direct the show. We become metaphysical megalomaniacs, as it were. Deluded by our visions of grandeur, we forget the purpose of our vision and get lost in false images of ourselves. Then, when scenarios don't turn out the way we have scripted them, we become disappointed, frustrated, and confused.

It is not our purpose to be masters of the universe. The universe already has a master and, if we don't learn to trust the intelligence guiding it, we become separate from our own intelligence. We are a part of this intelligent system, but we are not the controlling force. Our purpose is to learn how to master our individual and collective living. This involves knowing the limitations of our spheres of influence and the ability to take what life gives us and make the most of it.

Each of us has an "influential self" and an "influenced self." The influential self is the movie-maker, the mind-manager, and the CEO. This part of us can learn how to tap the intelligence and energy of the universe in order to produce specific results and experiences. The influenced self begins at the boundary line between what we can control and what we cannot control. Knowing the limits of personal power is simple wisdom or common sense.

For example, I cannot personally control the situations in Yugoslavia, Somalia, Tibet, or New York City where a terrorist bomb exploded at the Trade Towers. I cannot control volcanoes, earthquakes, blizzards, or hurricanes. I cannot control the Japanese economy or the European Common Market. I cannot control the number of AIDS cases, the homeless, or the hungry. I can pray for global healing. I can do my part to influence the whole. But there are things that are obviously out of my hands at present the time.

I once had a client who complained of a terrible toothache. He came to me for spiritual healing. He believed that he had the power to heal himself and wanted the correct thoughts and affirmations to process his pain and repair his cavity. So I gave him what he wanted and he went home to play metaphysical dentist. I didn't hear from him for two weeks, at which point he asked for another appointment. When I saw him, his jaw was swollen and he was in more pain than he was the first visit. I suggested that he see a dentist. It was a radical idea for him. He replied that it would be a spiritual defeat to succumb to the medical establishment. This guy had no common sense. I told him so. I advised him to work on his teeth affirmations but, at the same time, get help immediately. The medical establishment, I proposed, can offer wonderful support for our physical bodies while we are learning more about our roles in healing.

If you want to fly, imagining yourself with wings won't make it happen. And it would be foolish to leap off the Empire State Building to test your ability. At least begin by jumping off a chair. Be wise. Know your limits.

There are no stunt-men in the movie of your life.

As children we must learn boundaries. In the womb, when

our bodies are joined to our mothers', there is no clear distinction between where we end and our mothers begin. When we are infants, we still retain this vital intimate connection to the world around us, assuming that we are supported by a nurturing world which is safe and loving. As adults, we often forget this connection. But it is equally important that we learn separation, even if it's not ultimately the truth. When a child reaches his hand towards a fire, he or she must learn that it's hot and potentially harmful. He or she must acquire the appropriate boundary to be near the heat but not in it.

When the umbilical cord is cut, we are liberated to be our individual selves. We are also separated from our mothers and the security they represent. So we carry a conflicting feeling about separation; on the one hand, we fear it and, on the other hand, we want to be independent, self-sufficient individuals. The process of individuation is necessary, but should be kept in its proper perspective. We don't want to lose the primal connection to the universe around us, but we need to see our diverse and separate selves. It is by fulfilling ourselves as individuals that we can play a greater role in contributing to the health of the whole.

Let's turn our attention to money and see how the process of individuation applies. During the first twelve weeks of pregnancy, before the umbilical cord forms, we exist on the wall of the uterus. We grow from a single cell to clusters of cells into a little human form in these twelve weeks. Never again will we experience such rapid physical development. We do this without money, without food, without a job. Our growth is purely the product of intelligent energy, call it genetics or God, that guides and directs this magnificent evolution. At twelve weeks, the cord forms, and we receive our nourishment and oxygen directly from our mothers' bodies. We are parasites, living off another organism, completely dependent on its well-being for our own.

When we're born and the cord is cut, we remain dependent on others. Although we can now breathe by ourselves, we need our parents to feed us, love us, and teach us how to survive. It is as though we have just arrived from another planet. We need all the help we can get to acclimatize to our new environment. We soon learn we need our parents to work and make money in order to be able to provide for us.

As we grow older, we, ideally go through a healthy weaning process, which is physical, mental, and emotional. We learn what's ours and what's not ours. At first we want everything to belong to us the way we perceived it in the womb. It takes much education and reinforcement before a child learns to distinguish what's his or hers and what's not. Obviously, this applies to material possessions. Sharing is an alien concept for an infant. The weaning process can be even more complicated when it comes to thinking and feeling. It can take a long time before we learn to think and feel for ourselves and allow others the freedom to have their independent thoughts and emotions. Some people never accomplish this, especially if their parents never taught them this because they, themselves, were never properly weaned when they were children.

Many of us get halfway. We know we are separate from others, but we want them to think and feel the way we do. We crave that uniformity that made us feel secure in the womb. And we feel threatened by the differences among people. Rather than celebrating diversity as the spice of life, we are so insecure that we condemn everything different. We become narrow-minded, intolerant, and prejudiced. We think that the entire world is confused or crazy because not everyone conforms to our way of thinking, feeling, and behaving. In this movie, we project our lack of security onto others, blaming them for our own insecurities.

Meanwhile, our bodies grow older. We need to provide for ourselves if we want to survive, or so it seems. We need to make money. We know we have to succeed on our own, but, depending upon how we were weaned, we can be unclear as to how to go about it.

I always wondered why, as adults, some people remain financially immature, why they steal, lie, and abuse financial trust. It's no accident that we call it cheating when someone is financially as well as sexually dishonest. Some people are kleptomaniacs: they compulsively take what's not theirs. Some others are pickpockets, thieves, burglars, and bank robbers. Then there are the more professional crooks, "insider traders," wheeler-dealers, extortionists, embezzlers, and swindlers. These are individuals who have not learned boundaries. They are still infants thinking "mine, mine, mine." Perhaps they were abused as children. Perhaps they were neglected. Certainly, no one ever taught them why they should become honest, independent businesspeople. They know the law; they know the system; but, never having been properly socialized in their families, they could never behave appropriately as adults. They are not adults.

Emotionally and psychologically, they are examples of arrested development. They are motivated by their infantile needs, dependent upon a wealth they do not know how to create except in antisocial ways. They are actually cheating themselves, but they have no awareness of the price they pay for their ignorance of boundaries. They are sound asleep.

Most of us are honest. We find employment to fill our financial needs. But then we become dependent upon our jobs. We transfer our incomplete weaning and our unresolved need for umbilical nourishment, the breast, or our dad onto our jobs, employers, and paychecks. We live in fear of losing what we've established, forgetting or never having learned that we ourselves are the source of our financial progress.

Many of us form codependent financial relationships. We obtain jobs, perform very well, and try to make ourselves indispensable to the company. We think that if we can only make our boss need us enough, then he or she will be obligated to retain us, promote us, and keep feeding us more and more. We are still financial parasites, though somewhat more normal versions. The problem is, the boss or company might not see our devotion in the same light as we do. So when business is slow and cutbacks are necessary, we might be dismissed along with the next person, and be left feeling betrayed and unappreciated. No matter how much we do, it never seems to be enough.

On the other hand, perhaps we have attained a sense of boundaries and independence. This seems like the solution to our woes. If we don't need anything from anyone, then we cannot be the victim of other people's actions. We can respect their boundaries, and they can leave us alone. We can be self-sufficient, strong, and separate. After all, isn't that the ultimate goal, independence—financial independence? Yes and no.

"No man is an island," the poet John Donne wrote three hundred year ago. The problem with financial independence is that it can create isolation. If we are isolated financially, we can survive. For that matter, we can survive stranded on a desert island without any money. But is survival sufficient? What about survival with a great deal of accumulated wealth? Is that the end of the movie? Or is it our limit, given the nature of the movie?

If our purpose is to bring our movie into alignment with our vision, then we need to move beyond the limitations of independence. We need to remember the pool of gold in the cave. We need to keep the big picture in mind, the commonwealth. Once we remember the vision, we realize that we are unfulfilled being independent. What deeply nurtures and satisfies us is continuing our evolution and attaining a true state of interdependence.

We are not entirely separate organisms though we must learn to individuate ourselves. Once we have learned the lessons of separation, we must wake up to the fact that we are all part of one organism, life itself. We must learn to cooperate and support each other. We must realize that no one can thrive until all of us are well and well-off. Can a single cell in the body be healthy when the others suffer? If one cell is damaged, isn't it the concern of the entire body to heal it again? It's in our own self-interest to assume responsibility for the commonwealth of life.

This holds true for countries as well as for people. We have seen enormous changes in the political and geographical boundaries of this planet in recent years. Countries are groups of people, and the evolution of international relationships is an expression of personal relationships. How can countries learn correct boundaries until people learn theirs? How can large corporations go beyond the conquering mode in the marketplace when individuals are doing the same? Countries and companies will wake up to the value of international unity when that value is cherished by enough people. As long as we are trapped in the dream of independence as the final goal, we will rerun the movie of separation equals freedom over and over again. Revolution, overthrow, civil war, invasion, corporate takeover, and economic blockade—these will remain the fruitless expressions of countries, companies, cultures, and communities of people everywhere, seeking their identities in all the wrong places.

Freud said that true sanity resulted from the "reality principle," which he defined as the healthy knowledge of the objective and subjective, what is outside the psyche and what is inside. Contemporary ecopsychologists, however, question this limited view of mental health. They suggest that Freud was overly influenced by the second law of thermodynamics, entropy. Since Freud held this view of a universe headed irretrievably towards inert uniformity, he felt that the mental health of the individual must be based on separating from this cold, cruel world. Of course, thinking that consciousness was also an inevitable victim of entropy, he didn't see much hope for the psyche in the long run either.

Freud was not a spiritual psychologist but, rather, obsessively materialistic in his view of the universe. Ecopsychologists, on the other hand, suggest that it is the very separation of the self from the universe that Freud considered healthy that is the root of our eco-disassociation. Unlike so-called primitive people, we have lost our natural sense of unity with the environment around us. We have difficulty envisioning ourselves as part of the eco-system. Yet even Freud internalized the doomsday theory to include the death wish of the psyche. Ecopsychologists believe that the universe is friendly and life-supporting, and that when we see ourselves as a part of the whole, we are stirred out of our inertia into eco-action.

What is perceived ecologically is manifested economically. If we want to be pro-active individuals harnessing the wealth around us, we need to see ourselves included in that wealth and not isolated from it.

Boundaries serve us in the process of developing our self-esteem, our individual talents, gifts, and assets. As Robert Frost taught us, "Good fences make good neighbors." On the other hand, these boundaries are like membranes; energy passes through them.

In the final analysis, the earth is one garden, one market-place, one little corner grocery store. Earth is a family business.

♦ *Chapter 11* ♦

Taking Care
of Family Business

I know a woman whose father never wanted her. Before she was born, he desperately wanted a son. So deluded was he by his own desire for a boy, he was certain that it could be no other way. He lacked wisdom. Being a fairly wealthy man, he bet a friend fifty thousand dollars that he would have a boy.

When this woman was rebirthed, she remembered being in the womb, knowing that she was the "wrong sex." When she was born, it was a great financial loss for her dad. So devastating was it to her, however, that she formed a lifelong negative pattern. As an adult, she fell in love with wealthy men. Once they got together, his business would go bankrupt. (Obviously, these men brought their own scripts to the relationships.) This happened three times. Sometimes, she would try to avoid the "inevitable" by choosing men who were poor and taking care of them, but this was not the solution either. When she finally understood the source of the pattern, she was able to rewrite her script and change her movie.

This was an extreme case, but many of us have lesser versions of the same story. How many of us, for example, thought

74

we were financial burdens to our parents? Often, when couples are expecting a baby, they are both excited and apprehensive. They fear their own inability to provide. As helpless as a newborn baby is, often the parents feel equally helpless to adequately take care of it.

Consider the cost of raising a child. When we were born, the figure was lower, but formidable nonetheless. It's only natural that a new member of the family causes financial concern. This scenario would be more exaggerated if we had older siblings who were already costing our parents a great deal of money. Perhaps we were the youngest child and unplanned. Were we, then, an unexpected bonus or an unwanted burden?

We are all born into our parents' minds and hearts. The younger we are, the less able we are to distinguish between their reactions and ours. In the womb, we are telepathically connected to our mother's world. This psychic connection endures for a lifetime to some extent, no matter how independent we think we have become. Our parent's thoughts, feelings, and worries become our own. We internalize their struggles, dreams, pains, and conflicts.

A family is a business. Money comes in and money goes out—income and expenses. The parents run the company. The children are supported but are expected to contribute to the welfare of the unit. If we calculate all the money in the world, we realize that most of it eventually is managed within families. Yet how many families are aware of this? How many parents run their families as a profit-making business? Ideally, parents should have business meetings to plan their business. Children should be included in these meetings whenever possible. The family should work together as a business entity, creating a vision, long-range plans, short-term goals, division of labor, and systems of communication. The family should have a business account, a DBA, to channel all its money and to symbolize its financial aspect.

This is, unfortunately, a rare phenomenon in most families.

Usually, families sleepwalk through the dream of financial life. Parents work, children attend school. Perhaps they eat a few meals together each week, take an occasional vacation together, but rarely do they discuss the parents' work, let alone the business of the family. I imagine that most of us were raised by parents who rarely discussed the economics of their lives and only mentioned money when the children asked for more than they could afford. Then we might have heard warnings such as, "Money doesn't grow on trees, you know"; "Do you know how hard your father works for his money?"; "You don't really need that, do you?"; or "Who do you think I am, Rockefeller?"

We inherit a wealth of information about money from our parents. However, this information is often misinformation. We feed on what we learn, digest it and deposit it in our subconscious memory banks. When we are older, we find ourselves living in the movie defined by this financial inheritance. This is called family tradition.

Whether we like it or not, we have a tremendous loyalty to our parents, who are loyal to their own inheritance. Of course, many of us rebel from family tradition, but rebellion is not the antidote to conformity. When we rebel, we are still fighting something within us, and what we resist persists. When the children of the village decided to visit the Sleeping Giant, they immediately began quarrelling amongst themselves about the nature of the beast, imitating their parents' endless debates on the subject.

In many families, there is an underlying tension about money that, although unspoken, is detected by the children. They can be confused by this subliminal information because their parents might be saying one thing but thinking another. In my family, my parents would often tell me not to worry about money, that there would always be enough, but I could feel that they didn't actually believe it. I grew up confused about money and created the same reality as my parents. I always had barely enough and did the inner dance of worry.

Double messages are a disservice to children who deserve and need to know the truth. If a parent would say, "We're having a hard time now but, God willing, things will improve in the future," a child could not only cope with that, he or she could contribute more, emotionally and physically. After all, he or she is a member of the family business, too.

Of course, our parents protect us because they love us. They don't want us to struggle the way they did; they want their children to be better off than they were. And we love our parents. We feel sympathetic. We feel guilty that we are financial burdens for them. We want to take their pain upon our shoulders. What better way to do it than to struggle the way they did? And so we "mature," join the rat race, and try to climb the ladder of success. Little do we know that the ladder itself is part of the dream.

When we realize that our parents are protecting us, we assume there is something to be protected from. We forget the pervasive sense of well-being with which we entered the world. We think we are waking up to reality when we accept our parents' view of the world. Life is tough and we've got to struggle to make it.

We're afraid of failure but I think secretly we're more afraid of success. Failure is socially acceptable. Most people struggle and never make it. Most of our parents never reached the destination of their dreams. Failure can also be a way of getting even. If we were pressured to succeed and then received disapproval for our failures, we may have formed the twisted conclusion that the only way to retaliate for the disapproval is to do exactly what irritated our parents the most—fail. When we fail, we are saying spitefully, look what a crummy job of raising us our parents did!

If we are addicted to disapproval, we will recreate it everywhere in our lives. Our partners will constantly criticize us. The IRS, a great authority figure, will audit us. The police will give us traffic tickets. And our boss will always inform us of what we did wrong.

Many parents think they are disapproving of and disciplining their children to help them grow. But they are merely passing on the family tradition. The offspring of heavy discipline can be as damaged as the products of permissive parents. There is a balance. If we, as parents, remember that our children are human beings, deserving of respect, honesty, and tolerance, then we do them a great service. Their bodies and vocabularies might not be as developed as ours, but we should never measure their worth by their size or verbal agility.

Children grow best in an environment of love, learning, and listening. Parents grow best when they set a good example rather than demand that their children be what they themselves are not. Punishment can be counterproductive. We all deserve second chances. Telling children how to live their lives will rarely produce desired results. They need to discover their own way of life.

Scientists recently did an experiment with two groups of children from similar backgrounds. One group was told what to eat, given an ideal, balanced diet and not permitted to eat junk food, sweets, and soda. The second group was allowed to eat whatever they desired. Within a short period of time, the first group rebelled, sneaking off to eat ice cream, pizza, and chips; while the second group gravitated towards a healthier and healthier diet. Children often know instinctively what's best for them. If left to their own desires, they will not destroy themselves; they will flourish. Especially if we give them guidance rather than disapproval.

Parents need to be honest with their children, to tell the truth about how they feel so that when they overreact, they can explain why. They also need to listen to their children's feelings and establish emotional safety within the family.

The same is true of a business. If the executives and managers establish emotional safety on the job, the employees will not only contribute more physically, they will offer their suggestions for improving the business as well. Of course, if the bosses are insecure, they won't want to hear the good ideas of their "inferiors." They'll be too threatened. In a healthy business, suggestions can come from everyone because all are acknowledged and are essentially equal, even though the roles and salaries differ. A healthy business is healthy from the bottom up and from the top down.

A healthy family is a healthy business. Often children act out the fears and subconscious thoughts of the parents. I remember a time when my daughter stole money from me. It was a period when I was worried about finances, thinking I wouldn't have enough. I knew what my daughter was doing, but didn't say anything for a while. Instead, I looked within for the answers. I remembered times when I went into my father's closet, reached into the pockets of his suits, and took a few dollars from his wallet. Or times I snatched a candy from the candy store. Then, when I understood what parts of myself she was acting out, I spoke to my daughter and asked her why she was stealing. She responded that she wanted to take her friends out for Chinese food. I told her that it hurt my feelings to take without asking and that if she ever wanted more money and had a good reason, I'd be happy to give it to her.

Many of us were so emotionally abused about money as children that we have internalized this behavior. We have inner voices continuously disapproving of the way we handle money. We punish ourselves for our mistakes and, in so doing, miss the opportunity to learn valuable lessons along the way. If our parents took out their financial frustrations by beating us, denying us basic necessities or telling us they wished that we had never been born, we would naturally feel deep shame and guilt regarding money.

Often, children who were abused retreat into fantasy. (We may not think we were abused, but emotional abuse is fairly common.) If we are surrounded by a fantasy world, we can become confused about what we see. We may not be able to distinguish between the vision, dream, and fantasy. This reaction to childhood trauma complicates the movie, keeping us asleep in more subtle ways and making the wake-up process more difficult.

A fantasy has a different purpose than a vision or a dream. A vision is a glimpse into alternative reality. A dream is the unconscious mind's way of dealing with realities beneath the surface. But a fantasy is an escape from reality. When we're in pain, it's normal to want to escape. A fantasy can be a simple child's story or the child's fabrication.

As children, we fantasize about flying, being a prince or a princess, a cowboy or an Indian. My granddaughter is nearly four years old and she is one of the best storytellers I've ever met. I talk to her on the phone and ask her when she's coming to visit and she replies that she can't because her car is getting fixed. Or when she is at our home, she and I love to hide from the monster or slay him with our magical powers. Such fantasies are healthy, normal flights of fancy and they do much to develop a child's imagination as well as his or her power to influence the environment.

One of my friends has a daughter who is suffering great pain. She was committed to a mental hospital for a few weeks and, while there, she told her psychiatrist that her mom was meeting with President Clinton to solve her problems. This is a different type of fantasy.

When we have difficulty distinguishing our fantasies from reality, even when reality is a dream, we can suffer from escapist delusions. In the area of money, such fantasies sabotage success. We might think we are visualizing success when we're actually avoiding our fears of failure or attack and punishment. I've met many people who tell me they're going to be millionaires, movie stars, rock stars, or meet Mr. Right who is also Mr. Rich. They are not visualizing success, they are wishing it. Wishful thinking is reactive thinking, not pro-active. When we wish, we are reacting to a world we secretly fear, pretending we're on the verge of overcoming it but actually tottering on the edge of despair.

The main difference between a fantasy and a vision is that we don't do anything about our fantasies except retreat into them, whereas our visions spur us into creating, planning, and achieving. A fantasy, by definition, is an escape from reality. If it were to come true, it would lose its fantastic element. Sometimes we fantasize about things we don't truly want. We can have sexual fantasies, for example, which arouse the mind and senses, but if they actually happened might disgust us. Our vision is truly fantastic, but our fantasy is only an illusion within an illusion.

A fantasy is therefore just another way of protecting yourself from life itself. To the extent that you wanted your parents to protect you and they failed, you might make up fantasy figures, knights in shining armor to slay your dragons.

We all want to succeed. We want to put aside our fantasies and make something wonderful of our lives. Our family inheritance, however, can hold us back. We have a natural loyalty to those we love. And when it comes to our parents, this loyalty is reinforced by many years of bonding with them. To surpass our parents can be as threatening to our psychological survival as failure, even more so. We learned to survive in our family unit, operating within that structure for better or worse. Venturing outside that structure is difficult enough, but creating a new structure and succeeding within it is a challenge few people dare undertake. Many of us would rather sleepwalk through the old familiar structures, systems, and values, extending our parents' dream rather than living our own. The mind thrives on such familiarity. We know we can survive it, no matter how much pain it involves.

So we recreate our parents' lifestyle, ways of earning and spending money, and their ideas about money. Perhaps this is why the rich get richer and poor get poorer and the middle gets middler, as it were. What we focus on expands and we're often focused on the past, trying to make the present conform to it. How many people enter similar businesses as their parents? How many live in similar apartments or houses? How many pay their bills and spend their money with the same thoughts and feelings?

On the road to success, many of us hit the income ceilings of our parents, given the changes in the value of currency. We know, for example, that $50,000 today might have been worth $12,000 in 1950. So, we climb the monetary ladder increasing our earnings, until we flatten out at the ceiling that our parents reached. Not settling for this level of accomplishment is extremely important. We may be so blocked by it that we can't see beyond it, but we must keep on going if we are committed to the goal of complete success.

I remember the first time I ever received a check for a thousand dollars. I couldn't justify receiving such a large amount for a few days work. Surely, no one in my family had ever done so before. As I was handed the check, my body shook. I thought I was having convulsions. Fear and trembling gripped me. I was crying. What was happening? When I thought about it later, I realized that my body was releasing its fear of surpassing my family tradition. I was being healed of my inherited business limitations.

Later on, as I became more successful, I released another set of ideas I was raised with, thoughts about the rich that were less than positive. I remember my father's mistrust of the wealthy. "They're a bunch of crooks," he would say, or "He's filthy rich,"; "He's living on easy street,"; or "The big boys control everything." My dad was a professional underdog. I grew up with his compassion for the poor and hungry, but along with it I inherited tremendous negativity and resentment towards the rich. I had to learn to separate the valuable parts of my inheritance from Dad's prejudice.

We don't have to agree with everything our parents taught us because we love them. And if we disagree, we don't have to stop loving them or think that they will reject us. Even in the best of families there can be healthy differences of opinion. We don't want our families to become strictly totalitarian.

Anything unresolved in our family business will emerge on the path to success. Learning how to handle these thoughts, feelings, and behaviors can give us power, launching us to new levels of wealth. Financial growth always involves personal growth. If we're unwilling to undergo the personal stretching, we limit our capacity to receive. And the universe is blocked in its desire to steer more wealth in our direction.

Leaving our family's money tradition behind us is cutting another cord. It can be frightening because we are once again exploring unknown territory. When we were born and the cord was cut, we were both separated and liberated. The feelings are similar when we sever the invisible cords that tie us to our limited financial inheritance. It takes great courage to achieve wealth, deep introspection, and scientific observation.

When all is said and done, we may discover that the wealth we attained was not as important as the road we traveled. And that the movie we made was more of a home movie than we realized.

• *Chapter 12* •

The Value
of Relationships

I remember my father telling me never to mix business with
friendship. He said to do so was a high risk for both the
friendship and the business. My mother, on the other hand,
told me never to take money, or indeed anything, from people I
didn't know. "Never trust a stranger" was the message.

As I was creating the movie of my financial life, these two
bits of advice stayed with me more than I realized. And since
both friends and strangers were ruled out as sources of money, I
concluded that the only people I could prosper from were
"known enemies." I held a number of jobs in my late teens and
twenties to support myself through college and graduate school. I
worked at banks, publishing houses, schools, and colleges. At
each job, I subconsciously projected the image of the known enemy on my employer. If he was my boss, he was the authority I
could not like. He was the opposition, the system, the enemy. Of
course, I was also going through a rebellious stage at the time.

One professor supported me, even cared for me, more than
most. He guided me towards my masters degree at Columbia.
Then, when he became Dean of the Yale School of Drama, he ar-

ranged a fellowship for me so that I could be part of his new regime. He was a major influence on me. However, as soon as I moved to Yale the relationship began to change. Receiving fellowship money from him made me, in a sense, his employee. So, I unconsciously cast him in the role of the known enemy. Although he was quite radical in many of his views, now that he was the dean, the authority, he signified the establishment in my mind. I projected my unresolved feelings toward my father, money, and business onto him, sabotaging a wonderful relationship.

I don't believe in accidents. Somehow I was guided to my present business to open my heart, my mind, and my eyes. My business is relationships. Over the years, it has become obvious to me that when I do business with friends, it can be doubly rewarding. My business has helped me wake up from the dream a little more.

I also realize that the concept of strangers is a distorted one. A stranger is someone I feel strange with. The more comfortable I feel with myself in the presence of others, the more rapidly they turn into friends. Think about it. How long does it take for a stranger to become a friend? How many phone calls, cups of coffee or confidences do we have to share before we call ourselves friends? We can know a person for years without becoming friends. And we can have instant connections with people who become lifelong buddies. Friendship is not a function of time but, rather, of when we choose to open ourselves to someone, when we let down our guard and allow our natural connection to emerge.

You can love someone at first sight or spend a lifetime with a stranger. And there is no reason why we cannot exchange love and money at the same time. Moreover, if we do not allow ourselves to receive money from so-called strangers, we remove a great majority of our potential customers and friends from our sphere. We estrange ourselves financially. We deprive others of their desire to prosper us.

We need to realize that we are an interconnected family on this planet. We are a multitude of cells in one organism. Even those cells that are remote and, therefore, unknown are friendly in the sense that they too care about the well-being of the family. The health of an organism depends upon the harmony of its parts. The health and wealth of our planet requires similar love, caring, support, and assistance. It's ecologically and economically beneficial to take care of each other.

To sleep and dream of strangers is a strange sleep, indeed.

During my alienated years when I worked in theatre, I made many wonderful friends. I knew love was more important than money but, unfortunately, I believed then that the acquisition of one precluded the other. Consequently, I never made much money from my theatre work. I struggled a great deal of the time. I had fun and made good friends. But as a career, it was a bust.

Many of us mistrust the people we work for or with. We separate love and money, play and work, friendship and business relationships. We automatically close our hearts when we are at work. Why? What a waste of time. We spend much of our time at work with many wonderful people. We cheat ourselves when we block our capacity to love. Furthermore, to do so is unhealthy; it creates stress.

Sometimes we have "business friends." The people we socialize with after work or have lunch with. Then there are the "associates" we might entertain in order to solicit their business. But this is not true friendship. In fact, we often use the illusion of caring to manipulate prospective customers and clients. Let the buyer beware.

Perhaps we separate love and money because we're afraid that we can't have both. It almost seems like a sin to be both wealthy and happily in love. How many people do you know who are both? Yet the vision of true wealth must include true love or it's an incomplete vision. A wealthy world that is unloving is impossible.

Perhaps many of us exclude love from the office because we

think we won't be there for a long time and we don't want to risk loss. The opposite is true. If we place a priority on friendships, they will endure long after we leave a job. Moreover, it's good business to love the people we work with. Love is exciting. It galvanizes our energy and motivates us to accomplish more. And it also makes those we love work better.

When people are loved they are happier, and happy people accomplish more. It is very profitable for employers and employees to acknowledge each other for their good work. Verbal acknowledgment is a powerful expression of reward, sometimes more valuable than money. Many businesses operate from fear, not love. The workers are often criticized, but rarely acknowledged. They live in fear of making mistakes, which, in turn, causes them to shut down, be less creative, get less done. We can walk into some offices and feel a depressed, fearful energy. This is neither the atmosphere for accomplishment nor the environment for success.

The emotional climate of a business is of paramount importance. Not only should employees be acknowledged for their successes, they should be acknowledged as human beings. It pays to open our hearts to those we do business with. Sometimes, people come to work with hidden emotional agendas. Often they hide their feelings because they've received the unwritten memo that the office is no place for emotion. Nonsense. We all have upsets at home that affect our work. If there is no openness to share about these feelings, they will undermine all our best efforts.

It can be valuable to have sharing meetings at the beginning of each day. This can be done in small groups and need not last long. Nor does anyone need to help, rescue, or save anyone else. We can support each other by simply being willing to listen and care. Giving people the time and freedom to express what they are feeling will release the energy needed for creative work the rest of the day.

Recently, a friend and colleague left her job. She worked for my company although everyone is considered self-employed. I've known her for a long time and I have no doubt that she will remain a friend forever. She chose to leave only because the competition was too stiff in Connecticut. There are too many others here in the same business. The competition was too stiff. When we examined her underlying feelings, it turned out that she was the youngest in her family, the lowest on the totem pole. Then we observed that there were many other youngest children, including me, who were thriving. "Yes," she said, "but I'm the baby who never grew up."

Not only is a family a business, but a business is like a family as well. Its pecking order is usually modeled on the parental hierarchy of a home. The movie we create at work is influenced by our relationships with our siblings at home. This is, perhaps, one of the reasons we think that if we stay at one job long enough and gain enough experience, we will eventually rise to the top. As children we had similar feelings, at least I did. My sister was six years older than me and clearly had more authority in the family. I remember thinking that once she left home and went to college, I'd be number one, have a room to myself and more of everything.

Birth order can play a significant role in our business relationships. Knowing this information can help us relate to each other better. For example, the firstborn is typically the achiever, the responsible one, and often bonds closely with the father. He or she learns early in life that there are others to take care of, the younger ones. The firstborn often becomes a surrogate parent. He or she then assumes managerial roles later in life. He or she might become the nice guy or good girl on the exterior, but bear hidden resentment.

It's understandable. If you were the firstborn in your family, you were the only child for a time. You received the exclusive attention and devotion from your parents. Then, when the next child came along, you were suddenly assigned a secondary role, a supporting instead of supported role. You probably didn't like this new job. Of course, the new baby was cute and you wanted to play with him or her. But many times I've seen three-year-olds push their one-year-old siblings out of the way in an effort to try to reclaim the exclusive attention they once enjoyed.

Middle children are usually good at being in the middle. They can understand both sides of an argument. They can successfully adopt the role of peacemaker—the negotiator, or mediator of the family. They often have an extraordinary sense of fair play. However, they can be so identified with other people's positions that they get lost in the middle. They often don't know who they are and can have difficulty asking for what they want.

I've already mentioned the youngest children. The babies of the family often feel powerless in decision-making and are accustomed to taking orders from above. They don't like it, but that's their pattern. On the other hand, they can receive the benefit of having other siblings be a buffer between the parents and them. They can sometimes seem to "get away with murder." Perhaps by the time the youngest comes along, the parents have learned more about raising children. They might be more tolerant now, realizing that children often correct themselves.

The only child is, of course, a unique case. He or she is accustomed to being the one and only. This is the "lone star syndrome". The only child expects to either receive all the attention or needs nothing and is perfectly capable of functioning without anyone. The only child can have a problem with team-building since he or she never had the experience of being part of a team as a child.

Most of us probably never felt part of a team either when we were younger. On the contrary, the idea of a family being a team can seem quite incongruous. Most siblings find themselves competing with each other for love, attention, and power without even knowing why. Sibling rivalry is the beginning of the rat race we are expected to enter as adults. The rivalry and parental disapproval both shape the dream of conflicted business relationships.

In our vision there is unlimited wealth which we can attract for our own benefit and the good of the commonwealth. In the dream there is a scarcity of wealth, the source is outside ourselves, and we have to compete to win. When parents have a sense of prosperity, an understanding of the family as a business, and a willingness to include the children on the business team, the children mature as cooperative rather than competitive. More often though, the parents are worried about money, they hide their business activities from their children, and the children compete as if their goals are in opposition to each other.

We are taught that we lose if someone else wins, or that if we win, someone else loses. This win-lose mentality is painful. We either become guilty winners or resentful losers. Or we intentionally lose because we cannot stand the pain of success.

A recent study shows that children educated in a noncompetitive environment evolve more fully than others. When they are allowed to roam, meander, and discover along their educational path, they are more likely to develop their right brain as well as left brain in the process. They will eventually reach their destination but, more important, they will learn how to carve their path getting there. They will take more initiative and find new ways of solving problems.

Children reared in a competitive atmosphere might succeed academically and financially. But they tend to become narrow-minded in the process, obsessed with goal orientation, often missing the joy of the journey. These children struggle more, accumulate more stress—even physical illness—and can find themselves unfulfilled and frustrated later in life.

We bring the baggage of unresolved sibling rivalry from home to the office. We are jealous, envious, and resentful of others' success, afraid that it reflects negatively on us. Big companies compete with each other the way children do. Countries do the same. And so we have the rat race, the arms race, and the race to bury any perceived opposition. And as superpowers diminish their nuclear stockpiles, emerging powers, the younger siblings, seek to carry on the family tradition. International conglomerates gobble up each other like Pac-Man.

How can we ever have enough of what we believe there is not enough of? No matter how wealthy or well-defended individuals, businesses, or countries become, we will never feel satisfied until we operate from a broader field of vision than the narrow landscape of our dreams.

We have the power to change. We can take our vision to the global marketplace and extend love as we expand wealth. There is no ultimate solution except love. If we have the courage to create a true unity, we will discover a world of wealth in which we can all flourish.

If we want to wake up to wealth, we first have to open our eyes to love. When the Sleeping Giant opened His eyes, He smiled and extended His gentle arms.

We can and must embrace our vision.

◆ *Chapter 13* ◆

The Dream Team

A t the 1992 Summer Olympics in Barcelona, the United States assembled a "dream team" to conquer the world of basketball. It was an all-star team of America's best ballplayers—Michael Jordan, Magic Johnson, Larry Bird, Patrick Ewing, Clyde Drexler, and many others, fulfilling the "sports fantasy" of every basketball fan. Each player was the very best at his position, a superstar individually, and, with three weeks of practice together, the team easily defeated their opponents, and won the gold medal.

What does this dream of the ideal team tell us about our concept of teamwork? First of all, it indicates that we think the ideal team is comprised of ideal individuals in each position. Secondly, it indicates that, with these particular all-stars, a dream team is an inevitable result. Thirdly, it implies that a dream team would not have to work very hard to win. And, finally, it assumes that other teams would be easily defeated by our all-stars.

In the big dream, such a team is the best we can conceive. But let's analyze such a team in the light of our vision. Here we have a group of individuals highly evolved in a specific area, committed to competing and defeating all opponents.

I remember the National Hockey League all-star games I saw many years ago. The team that won the championship the previous year would play the all-stars from the other teams in the league. More often than not, the championship team beat the dream team.

I also remember the glory days of college basketball at UCLA, where, year after year, John Wooden coached his team to win the national championship. Coach Wooden had some excellent ballplayers, but not always the best. He seemed to have other elements, however, which were more important. These factors included a system that worked, a burning desire to win, complete confidence in the outcome, and players who were willing to sacrifice their individual statistics for the benefit of the team.

A few years ago I observed a different kind of team. I was in Kuaii and visited a Buddhist monastery. This was no ordinary monastery. It was beautiful, situated high in a lush canyon, overlooking the magical island. Twelve monks resided here. They appeared holy—dressed in orange robes, appropriately quiet and introspective. At first I thought it was just another monastery but located in a very special place.

I attended services, meditated and chanted, and was given a tour of the carefully cultivated grounds, sacred temples, and finally, the offices. There, I was amazed to discover a high tech center for computer operations which surpassed anything I had ever seen. This was clearly Eastern mysticism meeting state-of-the-art Silicon Valley consciousness...a perfect marriage of right and left brain functions. The monastery, I was told, was responsible for publishing the world-wide Buddhist newsletter. Each of the twelve monks was expert with the computers. Moreover, each was fully capable of performing all twelve jobs necessary for the operation of the monastery including: gardening, preparing the services, cooking and cleaning up. And they did just that. They rotated positions periodically—without interrupting the perfect expression of spiritual energy.

This was a unique team. This was not a dream team, a sports fantasy to entertain us while we sleep. The team was not predicated on opposition. Their purpose was not to win at anyone else's expense. On the contrary, here was a group of independent and interdependent beings committed to their own process of awakening and, also, to creating publications that enlightened others. I should also point out that this team was highly prosperous, as evidenced by both its lifestyle and its abundant equipment: top-of-the-line IBM computers, laser printers, and copiers. The members of this team possessed internal and external riches.

If we have a vision of an awakened world, the ideal team should include everyone. Of course, for this to be true, humanity must share a common goal, namely the well-being of the planet as one organism. Everyone must have a unique but essential part in the grand awakening. And, since it is unreasonable to consider a team of four billion people who can do everything, we must acknowledge our apparent shortcomings and reach out for support from the entire world in order to attain our common goal. A vision like this is something to strive for by building more and more effective teams whose purpose is not competition and conquest, but creation, cooperation, extension, and inclusion.

Jim Autry, in his book *Love & Profit*, suggests that we use the word "community" instead of "team" because a community implies common values and concerns while a team is premised on opposition. The word "community" has the added value of meaning literally "together in unity," which is the vision itself. I still prefer the word "team" at times because it suggests play, fun, and action. In effect, we can be a team whose purpose is extended to community. My business is called The Relationships Team, and our motto is "Everyone wins."

Individuals, countries, and businesses have often created external threats to harness their defensive energies. If we study the history of nations, for example, we see the repeated tendency to perceive the enemy outside rather than within. New countries,

especially, have projected the image of attack from potential op-
pressors, thereby creating a bond of fear among its people. Sometimes, this attack-defend mentality is consciously promoted, as
was the case with the Soviet Union and Chinese Republic. The
theory is, if you can convince the people that they need defending against foreign invasion, they will tolerate greater injustice at
home. The masses have always been manipulated by fear, and
only now are we beginning to see the possibility for a viable alternative. Of course, as superpowers have begun to let go of the attack mode, smaller countries and terrorist organizations have
been handed the torch—the knowledge of the power of fear and
the weapons to use that knowledge.

The United States has always thrived on this external enemy
myth. The so-called military industrial complex created enormous wealth for itself by propagating the idea of the cold war. If
you view it from the Madison Avenue point of view, the cold war
was one of the most successful advertising campaigns in the history of marketing. And from a Hollywood perspective, it was a
big-budget blockbuster, keeping us, the audience, asleep for another few generations.

Recently, I was in a taxi in New York City. The driver was an
avid Republican who began railing against the newly elected
President Clinton. He warned of a coming economic depression,
argued for the alternative of inflation, and generally expressed his
candid opinion that we'd all go down the tube with the new president's increased taxes, reduced spending, and southern hogwash.
As I sat in the back seat listening to this New Yorker's rage, I almost succumbed to the temptation to feel fear. Then I realized
that what the taxi driver was really angry about was his team losing the election. Then it dawned on me that the election cam-
paign had been about fear of change vs. faith in the future. The
buzz word for Clinton was "change." Change, change, change.
All his speeches seemed inundated with the word. And Bush
clearly didn't want change because it implied a change in presi-

dents. So, he was reduced to defending the past and appealing to people's fear of change.

How can we evolve if we're afraid of change? How can we embrace the new if we fear the unknown? How can we do anything but protect ourselves if we fear attack? Fear causes stagnation and financial paralysis. Fear at our jobs causes a drain in our energy and less productivity. We're constantly looking over our shoulders, fearing we've done something wrong, someone's doing a better job, and we'll be replaced.

Fear of economic recession or depression also causes financial paralysis. We think that we are victims of hard times and our self-induced victimization causes us to lose our confidence, imagination, and trust.

I always enjoy hearing stories of people who succeed in hard times. Despite the taxi driver's prophecies of doom, I personally do not fear hard times. I know, for example, that during the Great Depression, many people became extraordinarily wealthy. They did not enter into agreement with the world gloom. They knew that their minds were nobody's business but their own and they refused to be brainwashed by collective negative thinking. On the contrary, they looked out at the world with their eyes open and what they saw was enormous opportunity. Realizing the opportunity, they seized the day. While the multitudes were with the dream of despair, they envisioned a different movie waiting to be produced.

We shouldn't believe everything we read or hear. Most news reports are also an appeal to fear. Think about it. Newspapers and TV know that by focusing on frightening events, they will have more readers and viewers and thereby sell more advertising space and time, creating more profit. When will this love affair with mass hysteria end? When people stop buying the fear that's being sold, that's when.

A Course in Miracles teaches us radical lessons about fear. Probably, the most confronting to our traditional way of thinking is, "In my defenselessness lies my safety." This makes absolutely no sense to the part of us that is frightened. In our fear we are certain that the best offense is a good defense. We know that we need to protect ourselves from external threat and prepare for hard times. Yet, if the movie of our minds is a horror flick, until we give up the fear that we are projecting we will never experience true safety. We can be well-guarded, build body armor, spend trillions of dollars defending ourselves, but what do we create? More fear, more attack, more defense, more conflict.

In personal relationships, letting go of our thoughts of attack can cause instant transformation. If your partner is angry or upset, you defend yourself. We either justify ourselves or help him or her so that you don't feel guilty. Most replies in situations like this are based on self-defense. Consider the alternative: Your partner is upset and you don't reply, he or she will release the emotion and then it will be over. Most people simply want to be heard when they are feeling frustrated. They don't want to be confronted, changed, or even helped. They just need to express their feelings and receive loving support. A good listener creates emotional safety in a relationship. A good defender generates more fear.

The same holds true in business. An enlightened company will allow its employees to vent their feelings. Profit margins will naturally increase when people feel safe to be themselves at work. If we are forced to repress our emotions, we might transfer these unresolved feelings that are eating away at us into physical stress and illness. Then we are of no use to anyone.

If you're having a dispute with a business associate, the two of you can unilaterally stop fighting. When one participant in an argument stops, there is no opposing energy for the other person to match. If one person lets go in a tug of war, the war is over instantly. Try not to be threatened by different feelings and points of view. Remember, you are on the same team and the team can evolve when everyone feels free and emotionally safe. This doesn't mean that we should dump our emotions onto each other. Nor does it imply that we should allow ourselves to be a doormat. We need to learn appropriate ways of communicating intense emotions. If you're at peace with yourself, nobody can seduce you into war. Peace needs no defense.

Letting go of the dream of fear wakes up the team. The members, no longer threatened by each other or any perceived opposition, can go about their business of creating greater success for the good of the commonwealth. The team no longer sees itself as an isolated pocket of togetherness in an otherwise cut-throat world. There is no enemy except our own inner demons. The team has a valuable contribution to make, a service or product to share with the world which will, in turn, improve the quality of life on the planet. It thrives on contributing rather than competing. It can redirect the energy it previously used to protect, defend, fight, and compete and channel it towards loftier goals. Winning gains a new and deeper meaning, becoming inclusive rather than exclusive.

The dream team gives way to the visionary team. The team of children awakens the Sleeping Giant, who awakens the community to their hidden treasures.

• *Chapter 14* •

Cast Your Bread Upon the Water

Some years ago I had the privilege of meeting an extraordinary man. He was one-hundred-and-six years old. What most astonished me about him, however, was not his age but, rather, his spirit.

I was working in Montreal at the time. The one-hundred-and-six-year-old man was celebrating his birthday in a nursing home where I, fascinated by the prospect of life-extension, visited him. He was a small man with sparkling eyes and long, pointed Spock ears. When I first saw him, I was taken aback by his vitality. He was pacing the floor, unhappy and frustrated at being locked up with a bunch of old, sick people. He was in perfect health and accustomed to being physically active. Truly, he seemed like a caged animal.

When I asked him why he was in a nursing home being so fit, he pointed to the lady sitting across the room, his daughter. She was seventy-seven, but looked twice his age. She claimed that it was killing her to keep up with the old man and she had placed him in the home because she could no longer take care of him.

When I asked him the secret of longevity, he stared at me

blankly. I wanted to know if he maintained any special diet or ex- ercise program I could apply to my life. He shrugged his shoul- ders, having no wisdom to offer, it seemed. He ate what he liked, drank what he liked, and lived a life of pleasure.

I was about to leave somewhat disappointed when I noticed tears trickling down his cheeks...tears of love. He told me his life story and, as he did, I could see that his open heart and generous spirit were the source of his will to live.

He recalled the small town in Latvia where he was born, a town where everyone was a friend, where there was no fear and no conflict; a poor town of rich people and no hunger or home- lessness. There was one custom, in particular, he most wanted to share. Whenever a stranger passed through town, whether rich or poor, the wealthiest person in town would invite him or her to his house for dinner. A feast would be prepared and the stranger would be seated at the head of the table. Well fed, the stranger would then be shown to the master bedroom and invited to sleep in the best bed in the house. The rich host would consider it an honor to share wealth, even with a beggar.

When I noted the extreme generosity of his town, my one- hundred-and-six-year-old mentor, eyes now aglow with vivid memories, simply said, "We loved everyone."

Can an open heart and a generous spirit be the secret to a long, healthy life? Can giving freely, not from obligation, invite more wealth?

As children we are taught the virtue of generosity, but I think we are confused about the concept. Usually, we think of generos- ity in a condescending way, namely that those with more wealth owe the less privileged a moral debt. Or that one should pity the other, and give from pity. Nowadays, this idea is being promoted among nations. The rich countries should take care of the poor ones, it is suggested. In return, these developing nations should relinquish their desire for unbridled growth, which would cause greater ecological damage to the planet.

Being charitable has become a socially acceptable way of accumulating wealth. Whether it's signing charitable tax write-offs, creating tax-exempt charitable foundations or other imaginative tax shelters, or wealthy countries loaning poorer ones vast sums of money to buy their products—we see that charity is big business as often as it is an honest expression of true generosity.

Is the welfare system in the United States a charitable institution or simply the manifestation of a culture neglecting itself? We have recently witnessed the abrupt failure of communism as an attempt to spread wealth fairly. Both capitalism, where the rich seem to get richer and the poor poorer, and communism, where nearly everyone gets poorer, are based on the same insane dilemma, namely: How can you create wealth for enough people when there's not enough wealth to begin with? Once people succumb to such existential poverty consciousness, no new system, program, or proposal will provide a solution. True generosity will never make sense. And the spirit of commonwealth will forever be an impossible dream.

Are we doomed to always give only to get? Is "what's in it for me?" the best we can do? Can we only be generous from a mindset of guilt and obligation, pity and condescension? Or can we truly awaken from this dream of lack and mistrust into the abundant reality we have forgotten and forsaken?

As long as we believe that poverty is outside ourselves, that it is a social problem and an economic evil not a psychological disease, we perpetuate our denial by trying to sweep the poor further and further under the carpet of apparent wealth. As long as we believe in isolated individual interests, we will be unable to see the healthy and prospering power of true generosity. We will forever refer to our internal scorecards, our petty ledger sheets, and our annual reports, measuring how much we take in and how much we give out, and never calculating the true bottom line.

There is a story about a wise, old man. He asked God to please show him the difference between heaven and hell. God obliged him and guided him to a huge, golden door. When the wise man opened the door, he saw a feast inside. There were long buffet tables, an abundance of fabulous foods served on fine china, and a large gathering of people attempting to eat. The only problem was that the silverware was so large, the forks and spoons so long, that the food constantly fell off before it could reach their mouths. This was hell.

Next God took our wise man to heaven. It was the same golden door, the same feast, and the same long silverware. This time the wise man noticed one profound difference. Instead of trying to feed themselves, the people fed each other across the table, which they could do far more easily. This was heaven.

Heaven and hell...same place, different behavior.

We are at the crossroads of consciousness. One path leads to further and further economical and environmental downfall; the other to renewal, recovery, and richness. In order to proceed in the right direction, we must see the riskier path as a function of self-interest as well as commonwealth. And we must see the risks involved as unreal fears. We have before us a great opportunity to wake up from the dream of divided wealth and open our eyes to the unity of life on this planet.

Native Americans have practiced replenishing the earth for centuries. When they take, they give back, knowing that what they return will enrich the earth which will enrich them. The kahunas in Hawaii believe that every molecule is a living thing, every speck of dust divine, and every grain of sand deserving of love and respect. They advise us to ask forgiveness for all our trespasses, major and minor, over people, places, and things.

The reason it is important to be generous is that when we give, we actually give to ourselves. Sometimes people misinterpret this idea to mean that when we give, it will come back to us in the future. While this point of view is true in one sense, the future is also a function of how fast we clean up the past. Giving freely erases time, collapsing the past and the future into the present, which is, after all, the only time we can experience.

When you give someone a hug, for instance, you receive that hug now. When you do something to clean up the air, you give yourself a healthier breath now. When you do something to clean up the waters, you bathe and you drink in greater purity now. When you replenish the rain forests, you heal the ozone layer. When you restore the earth, you reap a richer harvest, yes, but you also make every season a wealthier one.

It is one of the ironies of wealth that we can only really experience it when we share it. Whether we give it away, spend it, save it, or invest in it, we only experience it as we allow it to be useful for others.

And when we enrich our brothers and sisters, we seed our own financial garden, we prosper our own financial environment, and we expand the wealth of our marketplace. The wealthier the universe that surrounds us, the more we experience wealth. And the more we enrich our world, the richer our lives become.

I once thought that I couldn't afford to be generous. When I became wealthy, I reasoned, then I'd give more. In the world of egonomics, my deductive thinking was quite logical. The ego is always reasonable. Yet, what was I actually doing? First, I was accepting my temporary cash flow, or lack thereof, as ultimate reality. Secondly, I was allowing my fear to govern my behavior so I was doing nothing to change my situation. Oh, sure, I struggled to make more money. And I waved the fantasy of future wealth as an excuse for my current withholding. But, essentially, I was choosing the reality of the dream as my field of vision. I was greedy and stingy, although I refused to admit it.

This changed when I met Mallie. When I moved in with her, I wanted to share more. The only problem was, she had two daughters. I was reluctant to share with them as well. After all, I wasn't their real father. What about child support? I was having a difficult time making ends meet on my own. My fear said, "no, no, no." My heart said, "go, go, go." And the more I chose to accept the entire family as my universe, the more I could see and experience that my generosity was my payoff, not my payment. The more I provided for the whole, the more I was provided for by a greater whole. I was beginning to learn one of the most important secrets of wealth—to have more, give more freely.

Receiving the generosity of others is equally important. To deprive others of the privilege of giving to you is unfair to them. I always had a difficult time with this one. My mother gave me so much—spoiled me rotten—according to my father, so that as soon as I was on my own I refused her support. I remember having arguments with her about who would pay for lunch when we went out, sometimes I would let her pay then slip a fifty-dollar bill into her purse when her head was turned. To receive her generosity seemed a sign of weakness to me. Perhaps I felt I didn't deserve it. Of course, I transferred this attitude towards others.

As I was writing this chapter in Greece, several friends started bestowing their generosity upon me. They gave me their car so I didn't have to rent one. They insisted on paying for expensive meals. It took some time before I could simply relax and enjoy the pleasure of their giving.

A generous spirit is a big spirit, and it takes a big person to both give and receive love.

There is a story in the Bible about Jesus being scorned for healing a man on the Sabbath, which was considered an unlawful time to work. When the people attacked him for his blasphemy, he protested, saying, how can you claim to love and respect God so much when you do not offer that same love and respect to the son of God in man? When Jesus made this statement, he was clearly signalling the most significant aspect of his mission, namely, to teach us that we should treat every man, woman, and child, every stranger, beggar, sick and homeless child with the same love and respect we previously reserved for a God we thought was separate from humanity. Jesus was a bridge for the evolution of human consciousness. Obviously, many did not receive his message and either branded him a sinner for comparing himself to God, or worshipped him as God's *only* son. But the teaching remains pure, simple and undying—we are all equally divine, worthy of love, respect, and wealth.

I think it was Mark Twain who said that the only problem with Christianity is that there are no Christians.

A Course in Miracles teaches that there are three types of relationships—casual encounters; longer, learning relationships; and lifetime associations. Each type is equally important because in each case you have the choice to share love and lessons or not.

When we meet a stranger in an elevator, or a beggar on the street, this is a casual encounter. We have a choice whether to project separation on this apparently inconsequential person, hide behind our fears and close our hearts, or open our eyes to an aspect of divinity that has been sent to us, a brief but holy instant of potential self-recognition in another.

As we give to these strangers, we give to ourselves. And so will we give to our longer and even lifetime friendships. For all our relationships are comprised of a series of such potential holy encounters. We can live with someone for a lifetime and end up strangers. We can meet someone for an instant and taste the divine.

If we treated every stranger as Jesus, as God, as we ourselves would like to be treated, generosity would become clear and natural.

Sometimes, generosity is financial; other times, it is not. Sometimes we need to say no to a beggar in the street, the demanding child, or the welfare recipient. If we are addicted to giving out of guilt and obligation, we will have to say no to others to learn how to say yes to ourselves. But even then we can practice spiritual generosity, offering a smile, a helping hand, or words of love. There are abundant ways of expressing generosity. Even "no, thank you" can be a loving response.

I often suggest to my students that they create a "generosity generator," a large jar that they fill up with extra coins and dollars—a place for spare change. Then, whenever they feel the urge or when the jar is full, they give it away to strangers. It is interesting to me that the words "generosity" and "generator" are so similar. Generosity generates wealth.

Several years ago, Mallie's brother who lives in Spokane, Washington, wrote to tell us of a miracle he had experienced. Duane is a very down-to-earth man, not at all mystical or prone to cosmic experiences. Yet he was driving down a main road one day when he passed a hitchhiker, a woman. Not in the habit of picking up strangers, he continued down the road several miles when he had a sudden urge to turn around and go back to help the fellow traveler, which he did. Call it a spirit of generosity, a moment of deep calling, a change of heart, whatever! The hitchhiker climbed in—a surprisingly beautiful woman. They talked for several miles. They talked about God, Jesus, and the Second Coming, which she said had already occurred. Duane didn't know what to make of this. When he turned to say something to his strange companion, she was gone. She had vanished into thin air. As Duane describes the incident, all that remained was the sparkle of fairy dust particles where the stranger had been sitting. Overwhelmed, Duane pulled over to the side of the road and wept from the bottom of his heart.

Who was the recipient of Duane's generous act—the hitchhiker or the driver?

"Cast thy bread upon the water: for thou shalt find it after many days," we are advised in *Ecclesiastes*. Yes, giving freely can be a wise investment in our future well-being. But true generosity is received the moment love is shared.

Chapter 15

The Power
of Gratitude

My mother always told me that I should be more grateful, but it took me many years to learn the wisdom of what she said. She'd tell me that some day I might be able to afford the best, but in the meantime I should count my blessings and be thankful for what I had. Besides, she'd add, "All that glitters is not gold." Mom was full of wise sayings, but I was ten and wisdom was the last thing on my mind.

I resented the fact that I should be grateful. It made me feel guilty for wanting more, seemed a justification for having less, and all in all, appeared to compromise my desire for wealth. Moreover, gratitude felt like a matter of politeness, manners, and social etiquette rather than a wise way of living. I instinctively rebelled against such manipulation. Gratitude was like religion, I reasoned, the opiate of the people. I'd be damned if I'd swallow such holy hogwash.

So, I fixed my sights on more and more unreachable stars, hardly noticing that my feet were leaving the ground. I was a dreamer. Like Nick in *The Great Gatsby* I window-shopped in the candy store of wealth, but was excluded from the sweets by a principle I didn't understand.

I was born quickly and have always been in a rush to meet my goals. When my dad would tell me to be patient or my mom would suggest that I might be a late bloomer, I would practically hit the ceiling. As if to prove them wrong, I would often attain rapid results. I could cram amazing amounts of information the night before an exam, and easily get top marks. I skipped grades in school, graduating from high school at sixteen, college at twenty. When I was twenty-two, I was married and had a masters degree. I could run faster than most kids. And I was always quick to reply to a challenging statement, the words seeming to fly out of my mouth before I knew what I was saying. But the price I paid for my speed was that I often missed critical steps of my journey through life, steps that I needed to take in order to wake up from my dream of deprivation, steps that I would repeat over and over again before they made sense to me.

Lack of gratitude kept me backtracking for many years.

I could never understand my mother's obsession with clipping out countless bargain coupons from the newspapers. Indeed, her virtual glee at studying these coupons, saving two cents on Clorox or three cents on Kleenex, often drove me crazy, as did her compulsion for counting pennies, nickles and dimes. "A penny saved is a penny earned," she'd say.

I could not have cared less about pennies; I had my eye on bigger stakes. I'd walk down the street, my head in the clouds, my heart in a fantasy of future wealth, blind to the gifts that surrounded me, my feet trampling thousands of pennies, nickels, and dimes my mom would have noticed and stopped to retrieve. Not me. Counting the little things seemed like a waste of time; time was money and I was in a rush. Besides, pennies were for the poor, the stuff of wishing wells not of dreams come true. I was not at all interested in small change.

In those days I identified more with my dad. He was full of

adventure, ambition, big dreams, and the promise of future wealth which, although it always eluded his reach, triggered my imagination and got me stretching.

As I evolved, I slowly learned the prospering power of gratitude. I began to see that what I was ungrateful for I resented and that what I resented was where I stayed. I learned that all there is in life are success and lessons, and that when I was grateful for every little success, I grew into greater successes. And when I was grateful for my lessons, I learned them faster and they also contributed to my greater success. Whereas I had previously been a know-it-all, the more I admitted to myself that there was a wealth of valuable lessons I needed to learn, the more I opened up to divine guidance. And the more my mind relaxed into the universe's desire to teach me, the more my heart relaxed into a spirit of gratitude.

Still, it came slowly to me. Slowly is holy, I learned, patience remaining one of my life's major lessons. At first I acquired what I'd call generic gratitude. I sensed it was a valuable metaphysical principle and allowed my ego to flirt with it. I began to express my gratitude more frequently to people. I found the words "thank you" easier to utter, whether I was receiving communications I welcomed or even the more difficult feelings people were beginning to express to me. (I guess they had always expressed them, but when you're as locked up inside as I was, there are things that are too threatening to tolerate, so you don't hear what people are really trying to say.) The more I said "thank you," the safer people felt in my presence, the more my relationships improved, and the more I prospered.

I always knew that I should be grateful to my parents. They loved me, made great sacrifices for me, and supported me beyond my ability to receive from them. But I often felt so overwhelmed by their concern, so suffocated by their love, and so trapped by their parenting that I was too busy trying to escape to receive the spiritual wisdom they were constantly demonstrating. As long as

I thought I should be more grateful, I felt obligated rather than free, and gratitude cannot be discovered in the pool of moral debts.

A funny thing was happening to me on the way to my awakening: I was becoming a happier person. And the more joy, love, and success I found in life, the fewer reasons I had not to be grateful. After all, we can't have it both ways. When we enjoy our lifes, our minds are focused on what's good. Instead of justifying our misery with a litany of complaints, grievances, regrets, and resentments, our immersion into present satisfaction seems to obliterate the past. Joy and pain cannot occupy the same space at the same time. Gratitude begins to emerge naturally as we have less need to blame and more cause to celebrate.

My path took me to deeper and deeper levels of gratitude. As I explored the nature of my dream in greater depth and expanded my commitment to living life unclouded by past projections, I discovered that I wanted to take full responsibility for my experience. I saw that I needed to be in the driver's seat in order to change directions and reach my destination. And so I vowed never again to be the back-seat driver of my life. No more victim mentality. No more reactive personality. At first I thought that I could become a pro-active personality from now forward. I avoided the rear view mirror. But the more I considered the entire journey, the more I had to face the fact that to go where I wanted to, I would have to change my past as well as my future. I would have to recreate my personal history at the same time that I was creating my ideal future.

The mind, I learned, selectively remembers. When we are unhappy, frustrated, or resentful, we remember only those events and our perceptions of them that justify our current misery. We blame our frequently distorted memories of our childhoods, our parents, siblings, teachers, and religion. We take these memories to court using our suffering as a constant witness. What we are actually doing, however, is taking ourselves to court and using the selected memories as evidence. If we can blame others enough, we can be proclaimed innocent. Of course, the procedure never works because guilt, even when projected on others, can never be released in the courtroom of the ego.

Forgiveness turns resentment into gratitude. The mind slowly shifts its focus, selectively remembering happier experiences and reinterpreting the unhappy ones so that they become lessons in living that we are now willing to integrate. The more we are grateful for our current happiness, the easier it is to see how everything that has happened to us was a lesson, even when we felt most victimized. And lessons are blessings. Here are a few extreme examples: I have a good friend who is a master bodyworker. Don McFarland is the author of *Body Secrets* and the founder of Body Harmony, a subtle, gentle, and unusually empowering form of bodywork. When he was being rebirthed, he began shadowboxing in the middle of the session. He lay on his back with his eyes closed, breathing rhythmically and jabbing at a phantom in his mind. After the session, I asked him to relate his experience and he told me of his war with his father who was a professional boxer. When Don was in the womb, his dad insisted on an abortion, but his mom refused. Finally, his dad took matters into his own hands, punching his mom in her belly, trying to cause a miscarriage. Don remembered his prenatal bout with his dad, struggling to cling to life, summoning all his will to live to defend himself against his father's blows. Somehow, miraculously, Don survived. He later became a boxer himself, but as soon as he realized that he was still fighting his father, he was guided to the healing arts. He became a chiropractor, a rolfer, and finally, the founder of Body Harmony.

When he finished telling his story, Don, who is quite formidable (and quite successful financially), broke down in tears. He realized on a deep, cellular level that he was now grateful for his dad, without whom he would never have been guided to his life's purpose.

Mallie is allergic to bees and wasps. One day when I was out of town, she was viciously stung in the eye and suffered anapha-lactic shock. Her face puffed up and her throat closed tight. She could hardly breathe. Fortunately, a friend was with her and drove her to the hospital. The doctor who treated her insisted that she carry a hypodermic needle of adrenalin with her at all times, should she ever be stung again.

A year later we were at a wedding on a boat offshore Manhat-tan. A guest had a sudden allergic reaction to the shrimp she had eaten: anaphalactic shock. A doctor was present but didn't know what to do. Mallie did. She encouraged her to relax and breathe, one breath at a time, as Mallie opened her purse, removed her hypodermic needle, and had the doctor administer the adrenalin. She quickly recovered. She thanked Mallie and everyone cheered. Mallie, no stranger to humility or gratitude, simply responded, "Don't thank me. Thank the wasp that stung me."

When we have a context for living in which every moment of existence is a gift, it becomes easy to see the cloud's silver lining. Having an attitude of gratitude is having a healthy financial dis-position. Success usually follows gratitude, although our egos would have us believe it's the reverse.

Once I produced and attended a one-year Money Workshop. There were approximately twenty of us there who began the jour-ney, although only half completed the course. The facilitator was Phil Laut, a wonderful teacher and author of the excellent book *Money Is My Friend*. We made an agreement with Phil that we would pay him ten per cent of our earnings for one year. This was based on the principle of tithing, giving ten percent of all we receive back to the source. At first it was quite easy to keep this agreement as none of us were earning a great deal at the time— which was why we were there. We'd give Phil $50, $100, $150 per month and he'd give us two full evenings of his valuable time. It seemed fair, even a bargain.

As the months rolled on and we continued to write out our checks, it became apparent that the workshop was working quite well for many of us, and consequently becoming more profitable for Phil. Powerful emotions emerged from the group. I remember one evening when a member reported that she had earned $30,000 that month. The workshop was obviously having a positive affect on her cash flow. Nevertheless, she didn't want to pay Phil $3000. She resented giving him such a large portion of her hard-earned income, even though it was still only ten percent. Phil laughed. He knew that the workshop was becoming a deeper success, evoking the basic resentment and lack of gratitude we have about wealth. The more the workshop worked, the less we wanted to share its results with the source. Not that Phil was the ultimate source. He was just playing that role to reflect our own internal conflicts, enabling us to see that the war within us between gratitude and resentment was the same war as the one between prosperity and poverty.

The more we express our gratitude in advance, the more rapidly our future blessings become current wealth. In the universal mind, time is unreal, a simple convenience of the ego's limited vision and its need to measure, explain, and control all phenomena. Manifestation is a current experience. Of course, we do have the power to delay reaching our goals. Our fears, mistrust, grievances, and our regrets can block us from receiving what has already been given. It is difficult to progress far when we have one foot on the accelerator and the other on the brake. But as we release the pressure that's stopping us, we can move toward the wealth before us. Gratitude helps release the pressure.

We think about gratitude at least once a year at Thanksgiving. We create a big feast, gather the family, celebrate the harvest, and give thanks. But if we only celebrate the harvest, we miss the joy of the other seasons. What if we approached every day as a day of thanksgiving?

When my dad died, he left my mom an abundance of broken dreams, unkept promises, and sizable debts. At first she was crushed. Then she was furious. At the age of sixty-eight, she was retired, tired, and nearly broken. Not one to accept defeat, however, she returned to work and to the money-managing habits I had resisted so much in my childhood. She counted her pennies, grateful for each one. She clipped coupons, seeing each savings as money in the bank. She saved and she saved, accumulating more money than seemed possible. She bought bonds and CDs and IRAs. She shrewdly studied the stock market and began to invest in it. She diversified. She bought utilities, market funds, and even shares of a Mexican telephone stock which I thought was insane, given the phones in Mexico. Nevertheless, she made a profit. Little by little, she grew her own nest egg, enjoying the process as well as the results.

As she underwent her financial rebirth, she became energized. She seemed younger, more alive, excited, happier. She is now eighty-eight years old and still a dynamo. One day, recently, when I told her what an inspiration she was to me, she looked at me with tears in her eyes.

"Oh, Bob," she said, "I have so many blessings to be thankful for, my children, my friends, my health..."

"Your money," I added.

"My money. I'm so lucky."

"Life is good," I replied.

"Life is very good."

• *Chapter 16* •

Guiltless Wealth

G uilt is the black hole of wealth, the cosmic drain down
which the best-laid plans of rich and poor go swirling
into oblivion. Guilt is the fickle finger of financial fate,
the sudden reversal in fortune, and the fatal attraction to failure.

Once I was railing against guilt in my typical manner when
one of my students stood up and objected, "What did guilt ever
do to deserve this kind of treatment?" The group laughed, but it
was a good question, one that needs to be answered as we wake
up to wealth.

Guilt, I often tell my students and clients, is the mafia of the
mind. It is a racket, a protection plan we sell ourselves thinking
it will defend us against punishment while, in reality, it height-
ens the fear of attack and is the attack. Guilt demands punishment and guilt is punishment: self-punishment, self-sacrifice,
and self-sabotage. Guilt is the envelope of our dark sleep. It is the
opiate of the dreamer. Within the Pentagon of the ego, guilt is
the best weapon, best ammunition, and best target. Guilt is the
grand delusion.

When we wake up to wealth, we must leave the nightmare of guilt behind us. And we will never wake up until we see, within the dreamscape, the nature of guilt. So odious, so pernicious, so sinister is guilt, that it slithers through our lives like the serpent in the Garden, tempting us with knowledge, wealth, power, and control while, at the same time, it steals, little by little, all that we truly value. Guilt is psychological cancer, a fragmented state of mind, shattering our wholeness into splinters of discontent.

Guilt is the conscience of the unenlightened. We are taught that a guilty conscience is healthy, discriminating good from evil, keeping our inherent beastliness in check, and allowing society to function in a fairly orderly fashion. Guilt thus becomes the glue of civilization, the devil himself masquerading as Miss Manners.

Guilt is the corrupt politician declaring that the only thing he did wrong was to get caught. Guilt is the insider trader, wheeling and dealing on Wall Street. Guilt is the unfaithful lover coming home late from the office.

The proponents of guilt argue that we are born sinners and must learn to repress our innate ruthlessness or we will never become healthy, functioning, prosperous, law-abiding citizens. Thus, guilt pretends to be our friend or, at least, a necessary and constant companion on the road to success. But, oh the price we pay!

When we are guilty, we forget everything important. We forget who we are essentially, our true selves. We disassociate from our loving, lovable, beloved self and enter the wasteland of separation. Once we form a secret alliance with guilt, we banish ourselves from the Garden. Why? Because the foundation of guilt is separation, and we cannot experience the unity of the Garden when we build our world on crumbling ground. We have chosen our own exile from paradise. Then we attempt to build a parallel kingdom in the wasteland. The ego becomes our government in exile. It convinces us that the Garden is the enemy, a constant threat to our separate creation. So, we learn to defend our separation and mistrust the commonwealth, the cave of endless wealth, resisting the love that would heal us of our psychic schism.

We can read this from the vantage point of guilt and can perceive it as attack and judgement and defend our skepticism and cynicism. We can think that these teachings are trying to take away what we cherish, forgetting that a loving universe is a generous one and never asks us to sacrifice what we truly value.

Beneath the foundation of guilt, we remain grounded in a unified field, guiltless and divine. We don't usually remember this spiritual subsoil, however; when we do, we feel even guiltier for choosing to be separate. Now we think God must want to punish us. Now we anticipate attack and heighten our defenses.

By this time we are residing in a living hell.

We have already attacked ourselves. And God has already forgiven us because He has no sense of wrongdoing in the first place. In the unified state of consciousness, even our separation is unreal, a projection of our self-delusion. But to us, it feels absolutely real. The universe doesn't care about any of this. It allows us to manifest whatever we think.

We think we are under attack. So be it. Let the war movie roll: struggle, conflict, hatred, revenge. Bombs away! We write the script, finance the movie, and cast the characters. We think we are bad? We think we've done wrong? We expect punishment? What will it be—a long list of debts? love's labors lost? disease? crucifixion?

One thing is certain. When we think we are separate, we cannot have it all. And we will, subconsciously, sabotage one part of our lives to pay for another. After all, pain follows pleasure, the good times can't last, and something always goes wrong, usually when we least expect it—or so the voice of guilt will whisper in our ears. As long as we maintain our guilt, the carpet we stand on will be yanked from under our feet, at least until we notice that we have allowed our feet to stray from the promised land.

There we are in the wasteland of our separate but parallel universe. As we survey the dreamscape, we notice other castles, some bigger, some smaller than ours. We stand guard on our turret, and observe that the world is like a vast chessboard with its pawns, knights, kings, and queens. Of course, we are threatened by these separate kingdoms as well as by the bountiful Garden we can't forget. So, we attempt to conquer the entire wasteland, secretly desiring to be the one and only fortress in the land. The ego seduces us into believing that we would be complete and, like God, the sole administrator of a unified land. In our nightmare, guilt would then reign supreme and permanently banish us from the Garden, from the commonwealth, and from ourselves. The sleeping financial giant within us would never awaken. He or she would be dead—if such a thing were possible.

In our society and, indeed, more and more throughout the world, there are two prominent classes of sinners—the very poor and the very rich. We crucify both. The very poor are the hungry, the homeless, and the hopeless, or, even worse, the creeping criminal pestilence threatening law and order, peace and quiet. We throw the very poor into welfare systems, judicial systems, penal systems, or out of the system completely. We exile them even from our kingdoms-in-exile, creating tribes of wayward, wandering spirits, haunting the dreamscape but undaunting our egos.

The very rich we castigate in different ways. We love to place them upon pedestals, then watch them topple. Our movie stars, sports heros, CEOs, politicians, royal families, mobster bosses— we toss them to the wolves of gossip and rumor, to the jaws of tabloid reports, TV journalists, paparazzi, and slick attorneys. We flourish on their scandals, their illicit activities, their crimes and punishments, perhaps thinking that their tragic flaws somehow justify our own imperfections. The humbling of the rich and famous helps us to forgive ourselves, or, at least, to convince ourselves that they are no better than we are. After all, any one of us might have our fifteen minutes of fame. There's nothing quite so satisfying as seeing a member of the ruling class confess a sin, say he's sorry or, thank you Richard Nixon, cry in public. The tears seem to wash away all our sins.

But what are the actual sins of the very poor and very rich? Why do they bring such dreadful attack upon themselves? Surely, if they experience punishment, they must be teaching themselves and all of us valuable lessons in the dynamics of guilt. They are, in one sense, scapegoats, but there is no such animal as a guiltless scapegoat so something deeper must be transpiring within them.

The very poor and the very rich are both victims of the mafia of their minds. The poor have innocently misperceived their natural inheritance. Poverty is unnatural in the garden. It only becomes possible when they think they are uprooted from the soil of plenty. With the poor it is easy to see how this separation is transferred from one generation to the next. Family tradition, conditioning, education, and cultural reinforcement conspire to keep the very poor in the dream of perpetual scarcity. But the transfer of powerlessness is only possible when individuals accept what is handed down to them. Occasionally, heirs to poverty open their eyes, see the light, and say no, thank you to their tradition, preferring to carve their own path towards wealth. But, most of the time, the poor are content with their unconscious discontent.

Civilization seems to prefer this mass hallucination. The collective consciousness thinks that there is not enough wealth for everyone to flourish, so the more the poor suffer, the more the rich can prosper. This is why the rich get richer and the poor get poorer. It is a self-fulfilling prophecy, individually dramatized by every sleepwalking dreamer plodding along on the dreamscape.

The very rich are also victims of their self-imposed exile. Yes, they have larger homes, drive fancier cars, wear expensive clothes and jewelry, but these treasures are gathered in the wasteland.

The very rich are guilt-ridden by their original separation, by their choice to abandon God and the garden in deference to a kingdom of scarcity, struggle, conflict, and fear. They know they have chosen an unjust world, and the more wealth they attain in such a world, the more unjustified their portfolios become, try though they will to defend their position. Ultimately, guiltlessness needs no defense. Guilt, however, hires the best defense attorneys money can buy.

When the very rich look at the very poor, they see their own fear reflected. When the very poor look back at the very rich, they see their own greed. We can never have enough of what we have judged to be scarce. The very rich and the very poor are finally both impoverished, if not spiritually bankrupted, by their lack of vision of endless wealth.

Often, we think we are not guilty because we don't feel guilty. Denial is one of the best blindfolds the ego provides. Guilt is not a feeling, but, I must repeat, a condition, a state of mind, often unconscious and noticed only by the negative results it achieves. As long as we experience any lack, attack, sacrifice, injustice, or punishment, we are living the dream of guilt. As long as we defend ourselves, we are attacked by guilt.

The most common way we can deny our guilt is by projecting it onto others. When we criticize, judge, and attack others, we suffer from the delusion that they are the guilty parties, not us. We further perpetuate the illusion of our separation, but the price we pay is increased guilt, fear, worry, and conflict. The poor blame the rich for their problems and the rich blame the poor. The powerless blame the powerful for their woes and the powerful blame the powerless. We can move to the most expensive neighborhood in town, never glimpsing the homeless and the hungry, or we can be so utterly destitute that we never reach a homeless shelter, but we can never escape guilt until we relinquish the thought that we are separate.

We can project our guilt onto the world or God, imagining

it's everyone's fault but our own. We can sleepwalk in our dreams, thinking the world owes us something and refusing to take responsibility for our own choice to leave the Garden. What more can God owe us when He has already given us the world? Not our world of limitation but His world of abundance.

When we begin to recognize our brothers and sisters as extensions of ourselves, we begin to lift the veil separating us from the Garden. We release the denial; we see the guilt we have projected; and we begin to develop a true compassion for others, which we can now see serves ourselves in the deepest sense. When we let go of guilt, we can innocently take responsibility and correct our error with the open heart and the helping hand of friendship. As we extend love and forgiveness, we spiritually cleanse ourselves because we no longer need to base our righteousness on the separate stone of guilt. When we give up the defense of our isolated fortresses, we begin to return in unison to the promised land.

We are all prodigal sons and daughters seeking a return to our home in the Garden, in the unified field. We deeply yearn for the well-being that can only come from the cave of the commonwealth, where the Sleeping Giant has become a guiltless child. We fear the return because it confronts so much of what we have built our lives upon. But the more we choose to trust it, the more we learn that nothing we value must be sacrificed, only our pain, guilt and conflict. And, as we set foot together on the holy ground we abandoned (even as we thought God had abandoned us), we can claim a guiltless and abundant wealth for everyone, realizing that our only sin was the original one of thinking we needed to leave the Garden in order to find it. Perhaps we will be so humbled by our return to grace, we will fall to our knees and, tears streaming down our faces, kiss the very ground that has been blessed.

Or, perhaps we'll just applaud as the credits appear on the screen.

◆ *Chapter 17* ◆

Guilt Is a Waste
of Time

*T*ick, tock, tick, tock, the hands of guilt fly rapidly round the clock.

There is so much that we want to do, but so little time in which to do it. When we're guilty, we can't give ourselves permission to follow our heart's true desires so we end up doing what we don't want to do but think we should do, relegating our greatest pleasures, as well as our creative money-making ideas, to the back burner. We try to convince ourselves that once we fulfill our obligations and responsibilities we'll devote quality time to our true desires, but somehow we never do. There's never enough time. New obligations suddenly appear to replace the old ones, pushing our desires, dreams, and vision further and further into some nebulous future.

The telephone is ringing as I am writing, but I am not answering it. Let the machine do its job.

I recently experienced a case in point, writer's block, I conveniently called it. There was so much I wanted to write: a novel, two new self-help books, a Broadway musical, and poetry. There were titles, outlines, and beginnings galore stacking up the memory of my word processor. But I wasn't writing. I was busy. God, was I ever busy. Between my travels, my family obligations, working with groups, and managing my business, I didn't have enough time to do what I most enjoyed, writing.

I told myself I'd take a month off to write, but I never did. I rationalized that I wasn't in a writing mood, but I was lying. I persuaded myself that it would be all right if I never wrote again, but who was I kidding? Writing is such a joy for me that, if I ever gave it up completely, I would feel as if I had separated from a wonderful lover. I am totally seduced by the process of creating something out of nothing on paper. I feel surrendered to a force greater than myself when I write, transported to a world of inspiration, ideas, and images. I am awake, alert. My senses are heightened. I breathe more fully. I am transported to a state of bliss. I love my life more and am better company. Give all this up? Forget it.

A fax is coming through, but I am not reading it. A fax can wait, can learn patience too.

When I took an honest look at my situation, I had to admit that it wasn't a scarcity of time or too much work that was keeping me from my greatest pleasure and most enjoyable work. I remembered when I didn't have the time but had chosen to write anyway. I recalled other times when I had put my obligations on the back burner and buried myself in my creative passion. So I knew that there was something else stopping me, something psychological.

I asked myself what was the true reason I was denying myself so much joy and excitement, and the answer came clear as a bell: I was too guilty. What was I so guilty about? Nothing in particular. Of course, I could come up with specifics, such as my mother being ill, business problems, friends who were struggling, and the state of the world. But the true reason I was guilty was just that I thought I was. It was my ultimate judgment of myself. I was guilty, separate from God and therefore, unworthy of my greatest pleasure, let alone profiting from it. Therefore, I had no choice but to work hard, take care of others, and postpone my writing until a time when I would feel more innocent and worthy.

I began to see that my guilt and self-judgment was causing me to procrastinate by sacrificing my spiritual and business purpose, that I was denying one of the greatest gifts God had given me, a gift to be shared with the world. I saw my guilt as supreme arrogance and stubborn refusal to do what I am here to do. I realized how much time I wasted by feeling guilty, time I spent thinking of what I would do instead of what I should do, time I spent spinning my wheels instead of taking journeys. I could see my life flash before my eyes and I realized that I could waste unlimited possibilities given to me.

Someone's knocking on the door. I should get it. I don't want to. Go away, I'm writing. Leave me alone.

I've always had it easy. My birth was fast and easy. I was wanted as a boy. I had the usual struggles and rebellions growing up, but I always achieved what I wanted without losing the love of those I cherished. Some said I could "get away with murder," but I always had a healthy sense of humanity. Looking back at my life so far, I have to admit that it was governed by innocence more than by guilt, that, in fact, it was the opposite of my own worst judgment.

I also realize that I have flourished in periods of prolonged innocence, when I followed my heart and pleasured my spirit, and that innocence inevitably results in ease and happiness. And when I was guiltless, trusting my intuition and moving from inspiration, I prospered the most. These were the times when I not only created the best results for myself, but also served others best.

My innocence is the source of my productivity, not my guilt. My innocence is my pipeline to all that is good and wonderful and spiritual. And the more I take the time to dwell in my innocence, the more value I create in each moment and the more time I have available, not to mention money and happiness.

Guilt is truly a waste of time. It takes us out of the present, has us stare at the clock to see how much time we have left, and causes us to kill time by doing things we later regret. As such, guilt is the great worshipper of death because only in death can the guilty mind find release and redemption. Only then will time stop and innocence, hopefully be restored. Of course, this greatest of illusions is the one that subconsciously creates the greatest futility about life. What's the point of living freely, fully, and innocently when the Grim Reaper will inevitably cut us down anyway? So, guilt becomes a death trap from which there is no escape.

Innocence, on the other hand, dissolves the separation from the infinite that tricked us into believing we were mere mortals creeping in the petty pace of linear time towards death. Innocence dares us to touch the divine and reach for immortality. It opens windows to infinite vistas and doors to eternal truth.

Guilt creates waste. Waste of energy, waste of money, waste of love, waste of environment, and waste of time.

Innocence generates abundance—of love, time, energy, money, and life itself. If guilt worships death, innocence embraces life. Beneath who we pretend to be and who we fear we are, we truly remain as God created us, as inseparable from Him as is all of creation. We are each a vital part of a wondrous, unlimited universe, and the more we dwell in our own innocent connection, the more we unveil the miraculous interconnection that binds all life.

Guiltless living generates the wealth and well-being, as well as the wonder and the awe of the commonwealth. The children encircle the Sleeping Giant in a spirit of innocence, unity, and love.

Imagine a world in which everyone was guiltless. Imagine a world in which love was greater than fear; trust greater than suspicion; a world in which the marketplace was a haven for honesty, friendship, and exchange of our most intelligent, valuable, and creative products and services. Imagine everyone contributing their skills to make a living and, yet, at the same time, pooling their god-given talents and gifts for the well-being of all.

Imagine a world of happy, healthy children, a world of enlightened education and comprehensive health care, a world where we tore down the walls of politics and used the bricks to build houses for the homeless. Imagine a world where there was no poverty but only wealth, where there was enough for everyone to have more than enough, a world where leaders were led by divine guidance, and where people thought for themselves... a world of peace and cooperation, a world economy, a global village of cosmic proportions.

What would we be doing?

Let's not punish ourselves for what we're not doing. Rather, let's use this meditation to discover a deep state of guiltlessness; allow your innocence to guide you to serving the world by doing what you love most and do best and therefore most deserve to prosper from.

Tick, tock, tick, tock, the hands of guilt fly rapidly round the clock. Meanwhile, the arms of innocence stretch freely towards the heavens.

◆ Chapter 18 ◆

Forgiveness
Saves Time

F or years I had a recurrent dream. I would see a beautiful, young girl sitting on a golden hill, her body twisting
evocatively towards the foreground which consisted of a
simple white Victorian farmhouse with green shutters and a rose
garden on the hilltop. Suddenly, three threatening motorcyclists
dressed in black leather appear at the crest of the hill. The girl,
seeming to recognize her pursuers, tries desperately to run away,
but she has a limp and falls. The motorcyclists rev their engines
and, trampling the rose garden, descend the hill. The girl's bright
but frightened Bambi eyes now peer out of the dream directly toward me, the dreamer, pleading for my protection. Then I'd wake
up in a cold sweat, thinking I should do something, not knowing
what, guilt-ridden by a message I could not decipher.

During the years that I was haunted by this dream, I was a
struggling young playwright and director. My male energy was
aggressive; sometimes frustrated, sometimes arrogant. My female
side was dormant, restless, seeking emergence and expression.
When I finally unravelled the dream, I saw that the young girl
was my crippled feminine aspect, my wounded emotional child,

and the motorcyclists were my angry masculine side. I, the dreamer, was torn by a deep division. The golden hill was the wealth the wounded but innocent female possesses. The men in black chased after it. The white Victorian farmhouse represented purity and fertility to me, and the green shutters symbolized healing and prosperity. The trampled rose garden was my broken heart.

I was torn between two worlds at the time, the simple, homey style of my mother and the wandering, explosive spirit of my father. I had internalized the conflict between them, my child's mind longing to lift their pain, reconcile their schism, and thereby release my own guilt.

I knew I needed to forgive my parents to regain my peace of mind, but I had no idea how to begin. Forgiveness always seemed like a waste of time to me. It never seemed to change anything. It felt awkward, artificial, and yes, stupid. Who was I to forgive anyone for anything? To forgive implied I had the right to judge, sentence, or pardon others. My father was a lawyer, but I was no judge, nor had I any desire to play God.

It took me years to discover that to truly forgive can both save time and generate wealth.

Before we can master the art of forgiveness, we must learn what we have the power to forgive and what we don't. We examined the dynamics of guilt, its subtle way of denying itself by projecting the blame on others. We cannot even begin to forgive until we acknowledge that we first need to forgive ourselves.

I remember one Christmas when I was feeling like Scrooge. It was 1977. I had little money, resented having to buy the children presents, and justified my resentment by railing at the commercialization of Christmas. Finally, Christmas Eve, I begrudgingly took to the streets with $320 in my pockets to express the spirit of Christmas to my family. I walked east on 106th Street towards Broadway, my hands in my pockets holding my money. Suddenly, I saw two young tough guys approaching me and knew instantly

I was in trouble. One pulled a gun and demanded that I hand over all my money. I stared at the gun and was filled with rage. The gun looked like a water pistol, but I didn't feel safe enough to test my perception. I reached deeper into my pockets.

In one pocket I had a twenty-dollar bill and in the other, three hundred dollars. My mind was calculating rapidly. Then, in a flash, I saw my lesson. These two teenage punks were angels in disguise, messengers from my higher self to my lower self. Without knowing it, they were waking me up to the fact that I could always afford to be more generous than my ego would have me believe, reminding me that my greed was just my guilt which no longer served me.

I started laughing uncontrollably. My assailants were taken aback by my unwarranted lightheartedness. I knew that I could have given them the twenty dollars and they would have been delighted. I also knew that I could give away the $300 and use my credit cards to buy presents. Furthermore, as I dug deeper into my pockets clutching the two choices, I remembered all the times my dad would withhold money from me and how I would sneak into his closet, stuff my hands into his suit pockets where he kept his extra cash, and steal what he wouldn't give me. All this went through my mind as I took out the $300, forked it over still laughing, and walked away wishing the two a merry Christmas.

My transaction with my Christmas messengers was an eye-opening lesson in forgiveness. I was able to forgive not only my apparent assailants, but myself for my stinginess, not to mention my dad for his tightness and myself for taking what was not mine from his pockets.

In the six months following my "tithe" to my messengers, I earned over $30,000, more than I had ever earned in that amount of time before.

To truly forgive is not to condescend from a pedestal of false superiority and pardon a sinner's wrongdoing. No, to forgive is to release the thought of wrongdoing completely. It is to see that blame is always off track, based on denial, and a projection of guilt. We only judge others according to our evaluations of ourselves. When we see that any apparent injustice is a valuable lesson in disguise, we can let go of blame and reap the rich reward of the message sent to us.

Forgiveness is its own reward. When we forgive, we win a multitude of benefits. We restore our consciousness to guiltlessness. We reclaim our power and regain all the creative energy we wasted in harboring grievances. We heal our body of what's eating away at us. When we forgive ourselves for judging others, when we acknowledge that we subconsciously set up a situation for the purpose of learning, it becomes easy to move on to the following stages of release—to give up the desire for revenge and to forgive the other person for his or her part in creating the upset.

It is practical to give up revenge because vengeance is both unhealthy and a waste of time. Even if we manage to succeed in getting even, our satisfaction will be temporary at best. When we seek one-upsmanship, we embark upon a path of endless crime and punishment. It is not a lasting victory because as soon as we win, we must defend ourselves against retaliation and our fear of loss. And our own anger, ill will, and desire to hurt others causes us even greater pain.

We have seen the folly of attack and retaliation on a global scale, both militarily and economically. When we choose to fight each other, we drain our resources from achieving our common purpose. When we forgive ourselves for our negative cocreations, we are free to create cooperatively, generating more synergy, which means more success and wealth for more people.

Of course, we must deal with our desire for revenge. We can't simply deny it, pretend it's gone and cover it up with a fake smile. We can try, but we'll be repressing our true feelings. We need to pound our pillows, kick and scream, play racquetball, throw bottles against stone walls—indulge our temper tantrums until the desire to destroy has subsided and true forgiveness has emerged.

Recently, I was listening to a sports radio show. Bob Costas was interviewing a highly professional baseball announcer, Tim McCarver, who had been publicly abused by an egotistic ballplayer, Deion Sanders. Costas kept pressing McCarver, who had been a fierce competitor in his days as a catcher for the St. Louis Cardinals, asking him if, when Sanders had assailed him, his manhood had been on the line and if, deep down inside, he wanted to retaliate in the moment. Yes, McCarver admitted, vengeance was in his gut, but, at the same time, he realized that the short-term satisfaction it would have brought was far outweighed by the long-term benefits of nonretaliation.

We don't have to react with the same energy as an apparent attacker. Think of Ghandi, who brought an oppressive nation to its knees through nonviolent resistance. He knew that the more we attack love, the weaker we become. A firm but flexible spirit cannot be defeated by an inflexible force. A mighty oak tree bends to the wind, but stands tall for many years. We can stay grounded in our guiltless sense of goodness, maintain our integrity and professionalism, and not add violent energy to a situation that needs diffusion. The more we relax in tense situations, the faster you succeed and the less we will need to forgive later.

Forgiveness saves time. It is an ancient proverb that time heals all wounds, but sometimes healing seems to take time. Forgiveness accelerates the process. It hastens the return to the Garden of endless wealth. It quickens the rolling up of the carpet of time. Time itself is so often the way we measure our regrets and resentments on the one hand, and our fears, worries, and anticipated punishments on the other hand. To the extent that we think we are guilty for past mistakes, we fear the future as a time for judgment and recrimination. When we forgive the dream of separation, scarcity, struggle, and guilt, we often experience a sudden windfall from the promised land.

Furthermore, what remains unforgiven we are doomed to repeat again and again, the universe giving us ample opportunities to awaken from the dream. When, for example, I was unable to forgive my father for dying suddenly and abandoning my mother with broken promises and unpaid bills, I subconsciously attracted other losses into my life. A pattern appeared in my life of men I loved dearly, friends and colleagues, suddenly leaving me, even dying. Each time I suffered such a loss, my heart would open more until finally, one day in Bali, eighteen years after my dad's death, I felt the greatest loss of all. My best friend, Bob Phibbs, died in a tragic crash of an ultralight aircraft.

The grief was overwhelming. I was called upon to conduct a series of ceremonies at the crash site on the beach, the local temple, the crematorium furnace, and then when I took his ashes into my hands and released them into the Indian Ocean. I sobbed uncontrollably for three days, on and off for more than a year. I knew that it was not just Bob Phibbs I was mourning, but a host of men who had loved me and left me, leading back to my dad, for whom I finally let the bell toll.

Forgiveness wipes the slate clean. It erases time, space, and separation. When the children go to wake the Sleeping Giant, they do so to awaken their parents from their dream. They could have blamed their parents, taken on their pain and behavior, sleepwalking through the same dreamscape. Instead, they summoned the necessary spiritual courage to confront the source of the fear, namely the separation from the cave and the Giant who guarded the gold.

Above all, forgiving our fathers and mothers will generate greater wealth. Our fathers and mothers were our providers and nourishers, no matter how well or poorly they performed their roles. If our relationship with them is incomplete, our well-being is stagnated. What we resent in them distances us from our own capacity to nourish and provide for ourselves.

Within each of us lies a generous father and a loving mother waiting to be set free to prosper our inner child. We can control the time it takes. We can delay the forgiveness. We can even struggle to succeed at their expense—to show them we don't need them and avenge the wrongdoings we hold against them. But, ultimately, we will only wake up to true and everlasting wealth, well-being, and satisfaction the day we forgive them. In a flash, we will look at our past and see the perfection of we parents you chose. We will selectively remember the love they gave, the best efforts they made, and let bygones be bygones. Our hearts will then be open to the blessing of true richness.

My father died in debt, prompting me to study the psychology of debt and credit. We have debts to pay along the road to wealth. But debts are often misunderstood as guilts and obligations we resent rather than an expression of gratitude. We must forgive this misperception of debt or we will amass greater and greater psychological indebtedness in our lives.

A debt is a measure of trust. When we borrow and, therefore, owe people money, or they us, what is implied? Firstly, we, or they, are trustworthy. There is an assessment made that the borrower can pay back the money. If there is interest involved, the loan is seen as a good investment. Moreover, the lender and the borrower agree that the time of repayment is sufficient to create the necessary wealth. Time is on our side. We have faith in the future.

So, debt, which is synonymous with credit, can be a healthy financial technique for teaching us innocence. If we are innocent, we anticipate a successful future. When we are guilty, we expect the worst. We, therefore, accumulate excessive debts, compulsively mismanage our money, and keep ourselves in debt so we can feel more guilty. This is why debt should never be accompanied by guilt.

Often, when people borrow money from me and they can't pay me back, they stop communicating. A friendship can be lost if the debtor is so embarrassed by his financial plight that he cannot bear to tell his friend. We should never measure our self-esteem, innocence, or guilt, by our cash flow. Who we are is of permanent and lasting value no matter how great the fluctuation in our financial fortunes. Never let a debt interfere with love, communication, and relationships.

In God's mind, all our debts are forgiven because from the point of view of eternity—past, present, and future are forever here and now. So, the more we align ourselves with the eternal banker, the more we are able to play the money game with endless wealth as our source. Guiltless and connected, we can be faithful to our true value.

Recently, my recurrent dream returned. This time, the young crippled girl was healed and stood in a beautiful, white gown on her golden hill, a bouquet of flowers in her hands she had gathered. Her farmhouse was buzzing with activity, happy adults and children in the midst of celebration. The rose garden was flourishing. Birds were flying about. A full rainbow arched across the hill. The three motorcyclists appeared on the crest of the hill now wearing black tuxedos. They stopped their bikes and turned off their engines. The girl turned towards them, arms spread in welcome. One motorcyclist ran down the hill towards her. They embraced. They walked arm in arm towards me, the dreamer, with a procession of jubilant people following. As they approached me, I recognized their faces—my mom and my dad, as they had looked in their prime.

◆ *Chapter 19* ◆

Measuring Profits
& Losses

In June 1992, Mallie and I led a Loving Relationships Training (LRT) in Galithea, Spain. It was one of the most beautiful locations we had ever visited—white sandy beaches, the pounding force of the easternmost Atlantic Ocean thrusting against rocky reefs, the lush and generous vegetation, and, just a few kilometers inland, spectacular forests of eucalyptus trees and, suddenly, gracious mountains stretching towards Portugal.

The hotel was the flagship of the Paradors, nearly all of them renovated old monasteries, castles, and forts. This particular one was even more sensational than the others, strutting its ancient walls and verdant gardens in a sliver of peninsula, knifing into the Atlantic. Once a haven for pirates, it had been transformed into a peaceful palace of exquisite quality. Moreover, we were blessed with the Presidential Suite as our sleeping quarters.

The meeting room was a true gift. Spacious and light, with high ceilings, abundant and tall windows, and constant sea breezes, it jutted westward like a huge boat sailing to America. And the training itself, perhaps infused with the romantic nature of its location, was exceptionally sweet, deep, and unusually magical.

In fact, the only problem with the entire weekend was that the producers lost a substantial sum of money.

Adolfo and Carmen had been dear friends of ours for several years. They were a stunningly attractive couple who had been together for nine years and were parents of a beautiful six-year-old daughter, Sua. They were pioneers in the healing arts movement in Spain. Financial loss had never been an issue for them, so the results in Galithea were somewhat confusing and disappointing for all of us.

Adolfo and I were and are very close, like brothers. He and Carmen had been struggling with their relationship for several years, drawn to the LRT as a vehicle for healing themselves as well as for serving others. However, no matter how many seminars they took or counselling sessions they received, nothing worked for long. They were at a crossroads, trying to decide whether their marriage was salvageable or it was time to let go and change the form of their relationship.

In April, two months prior to the LRT, Adolfo had come to America to participate in a six-month program Mallie and I conducted. He had worked hard for many years and wanted this time for his personal renewal as well as greater clarity about his relationship. Carmen ran the business in his absence, supporting Adolfo financially and spiritually as best she could. Adolfo returned to Spain a week before the training.

Afterwards, Adolfo confessed to me that he was very tempted to blame Carmen for the financial problems of the business in Spain. After all, he was in America and she was in charge. She didn't do what she had promised. I listened to him vent his feelings. I didn't say a word. Finally, after he had released his frustration, he turned to me and said, "You know, Bob, I don't really consider this a loss. In one sense, it seems like a loss, a clear consequence of the loss in my relationship with Carmen. But in the deeper sense, it is not a loss."

He explained what he meant. He didn't accept the notion of

financial loss. In his view, this was one training in a series of events that comprised a year of carefully-planned activity. From the limited perspective of a weekend seminar, it might look like a failure, but when incorporated into the bigger picture of the entire year, the perception might be quite different.

He outlined his profits. Firstly, the quality of the training itself, he believed, would attract future quantity of attendants. Many of the graduates were eager to attend advanced workshops. Secondly, the public relations value of a training of such exquisite and exotic flavor could not be measured in pesetas. Word-of-mouth advertising, the most valuable in our business, would be extensive. Furthermore, there were deeper, more personal profits on which he could not put a price tag. Galithea itself was a place of fond childhood memories for Adolfo. Coming home to this part of his motherland had helped him reconcile with his family, a major goal in crossing the ocean to the six-month program. Sometimes we go a long way out of our way to find the shortcut home.

As Adolfo continued to enumerate his profits, including his reunion with his daughter Sua, the pleasure of being with Mallie and me, and the letting go of the old form of his relationship with Carmen, I realized that here was a man who would always be a winner. His optimism, his trust, his tendency to focus on meaningful rewards rather than superficial statistics would always generate success, if not resulting in immediate financial profits, then lessons and invisible wins that would pave the way to long-lasting well-being. Adolfo was not a man to regret or worry. He was, and is, too busy thinking about his next creation.

How do we measure our profits and losses? The question asks us to review our value systems. What are the rewards we truly desire as opposed to the ones we are headed for? Often, we assume that an abundance of financial wealth will automatically make us feel secure and satisfied. Granted, it won't hurt. But when we think of what money can buy—cars, houses, clothes, jewels, travel, or even accumulated savings and investments—

do we include the way we want to feel on the list? Of course, there is the flood of energy that can accompany a financial victory or expensive purchase. But the feelings of financial conquest are more what Dr. Paul Pearsall calls "junk feelings" than genuine emotions, which, like junk food can taste great at first but leave a greasy aftertaste in our mouths and a hollow craving in our guts.

No, what we truly hunger for are the rewards of spirit—the love, happiness, peace, safety, health, and joy that make life worth living. And these profits are beyond the purchasing power of money. A true prosperity consciousness is the ability to experience the physical universe as a comfortable, convenient, easy, and pleasurable place to play and grow. We can develop this consciousness at any point in our evolution, but, surely, no amount of financial success will automatically translate into this state of mind. We can be poor and think rich, or be rich and think poor. It's debatable which is preferable. When we wake up, we'll find ourselves truly rich.

Adolfo was demonstrating that we never lose anything, only make room for something more valuable. This might seem like a difficult statement to accept. We devote so much of our time, energy, and effort to clutching onto the past so we won't have to face our fear of the future. We compulsively plan our futures to protect us from our fear of change. We are more governed by separation anxiety than we like to admit, afraid that our jobs, homes, and loved ones will suddenly be snatched away from us. Perhaps we are terrified of cutting cords due to our first experience of separation at birth. The very thought of letting go can shorten our breath and weaken our knees. We are fascinated by but terrified of the unknown, confusing it with death, driven by the primal mistrust of being out of control and under attack. These subconscious factors can cause us to settle for less than life has to offer, believing that the security of having less is preferable to risking total loss, thereby missing the experience of true wealth and well-being.

I remember when my former mother-in-law demonstrated a classic case of letting go jitters. We were at a Werner Erhard Money Evening in San Francisco. Nancy was extremely prosperous, but she lacked trust. There were three hundred people standing up and throwing crumpled bills, the largest they were willing to part with, around the room. The object was to pick up any bills that landed in your vicinity and throw them away as quickly as possible. The energy was overwhelming. In the middle of this chaos, I noticed Nancy out of the corner of my eye. She was standing with an arm in midair. Her hand held a dollar bill tightly in her fist. She kept bringing the arm forward as if to throw the dollar, but her fist was a knot and she wouldn't let go. Her arm kept moving back and forth, back and forth. This memory lingers and demonstrates the paralysis of needlessly holding on.

I have developed a few healthy habits to counteract my fear of running out of money. The first is, I spend money when I think I can't afford to. I buy myself, my wife, my children, or my grandchildren a present. I choose to keep money moving in a generous fashion, priming the pump even when I think the well might run dry. Secondly, I hide money from myself, usually in pockets. Often, when Mallie is doing the laundry, she'll find a small wad in this pocket or that, or when I put on a jacket I haven't worn in a while, I'll stuff my hands into a few fives, tens, or twenties. Thirdly, I carry a one-hundred-dollar bill in my wallet at all times, just so I know it's there.

Often, loss will teach us important lessons, no matter how much we try to resist them. In 1973, when my father died, I was in Mexico, unaware of what happened and unable to attend the funeral. My need to mourn was repressed. In the three years following I suffered repeated loss. My marriage failed, my career stalled, and my house burned down. All my valuable possessions and writings turned to ash. By 1976, I was thirty-three and totally destitute. I remember walking aimlessly down the streets of San Francisco one night, sobbing convulsively from the depths of my soul. Was it for my wife, my house, my career, or my father that I was grieving? Looking back I would say that it was for all of them and none of them. I was in mourning for myself, my life, my mortality, which these compounded losses had evoked for my healing. This was the year of my personal rebirth, a time for releasing the past, surrendering to God's will or the way of my life, whichever, and for embracing the vision of my future. It was the worst of times and the best of times. And what followed was a period of enormous growth, love, and prosperity.

Emptiness is the womb of abundance. Solitude can be the catalyst for reunion. Nature abhors a vacuum, and when we are willing to empty ourselves of our pasts we are often rewarded with the birth of new perspectives and wonderful surprises.

When we discover our desire for deeper profits, greater successes, and permanent wealth, we undergo profound spiritual reorientation. We shift our values, clarify what's worth trusting, and relinquish our isolation.

In the course of making these changes, we are apt to feel that a sacrifice is necessary. Our egos would have us believe that a spiritual life involves the loss of truly valuable goods, that God wants to take away the possessions, places and people that we love and commands us to love him soley. Although nothing could be further from the truth, this is an extremely powerful misconception. It can cause us to hold onto our values even if we no longer really value them. We can become paranoid thinking that God wants to punish us and forget that what is being offered is far greater than any ego gratification.

Once I lost $10,000. I had secretly hidden it in a drawer. Mallie and I were in Europe for a month and when we returned, our house in New York City had been burglarized, and the $10,000 was gone. At first, I was devastated. Then I realized that this was the secret money that I hid from Mallie. In fact, it was my separation insurance should the relationship end. When I saw that the universe could no longer support my plan for separation,

I viewed the $10,000 as a small price to pay. Of course, if I had put it in the money pool I shared with Mallie in the first place, it would have been a far less expensive lesson.

In evolving a new trust, we surely must sort out our values and priorities, deciding what we truly value at this stage of our lives and what has served us in the past but has now become valueless. This can be a confusing process, but when we decide what is important and what is not, we realize that the only sacrifice that is truly required is the relinquishing of what we no longer value. When *A Course in Miracles* suggests, "I will not value what is valueless," it is not demanding that we make a real sacrifice, only an unreal one. In other words, we need to acknowledge that we won't defend what we don't want.

The material benefits of life are like icing on the cake. When we realize that it is the cake that nourishes us, that it is the spirit that feeds our deepest hunger, we can feed ourselves a healthy life and enjoy the icing for what it is. We make the shift—our perspective changes, our values are sorted out—and we begin to know that the universe is more generous than we ever imagined. We can have our cake and eat it, icing and all.

In *Ecclesiastes* the question is posed:

What profit a man of all his labor which he takes under the sun? One generation passes away and another generation comes: but the earth abides forever. The sun also arises and the sun goes down, and hastens to his place where he arose. The wind goes toward the south and turns about into the north; it whirles about continually, and the wind returns again according to his circuit. All the rivers run into the sea, yet the sea is not full; unto the place where the rivers come, there they return again!

What is the lesson here? On the superficial level, the message is filled with despair. Never count your profits because in the long run, you'll lose them anyway. Even your health, wisdom, and knowledge amount to nothing. "All is vanity and vexation of spirit." But so it is in the world of egonomics. When the Giant is asleep, we're all on cruise-control.

The deeper meaning, however, is that the Source abides forever. The world of our perceptions may be filled with cycles: profits and losses, pleasure and pain, knowledge and ignorance, health and sickness, life and death. But the world of absolute truth is timeless and everlasting, and when we establish and maintain our internal connection with the Source, we are not victims of the world we see. We can be safe within the dream. We can endure the changes in our fortune. We can even prevail.

In June 1993, one year after the apparent loss in Galithea, Mallie and I returned to Spain to lead another LRT. Adolfo greeted us at the airport and we could see from his face that things were going well. Indeed, this time the training was a success in every way. Many, many people; many, many pesetas. Adolfo and Carmen were living apart, but their friendship was closer than their marriage had been. Their daughter Sua was happy to see her parents at peace.

The hotel was outside Madrid and very comfortable: green lawns, wonderful terraces, and a swimming pool. The training was easier and more fun than ever, the participants seeming more ready for change than before. Many were graduates from Galithea who returned to continue their journey. All in all, there was no downside to this LRT.

After the training, Adolfo and I were driving together to the bank. He smiled and said to me, "You know, Bob, this success is a consequence of what we did in Galithea one year ago. So, who is to say which was the greater success?"

When it comes to profits and losses, remember, never count your chickens before they hatch. And, even after they hatch, if the profit looks insufficient, take a breath, relax, and thank God, knowing there's always more chickens where those came from.

Chapter 20

The Real Cost
of Living

I n June 1993, scientists reported that they had discovered DNA from a weevil over 120 million years old. They retrieved the hardy genetic link from an ancient piece of amber in Lebanon. This made me wonder how much the DNA was worth in today's market.

Many things increase their value with age—wines and gems, paintings and manuscripts, baseball cards and comic books, not to mention antediluvian artifacts. We can make a fortune investing wisely in the past. The more precarious our future seems to be, the more precious our antiques and relics are deemed, almost implying that we have left the best behind.

On the other hand, we can also reap great profits by investing in futures, be they grains, commodities, stocks, real estate, gold, the lottery, or the over-under on the Super Bowl. Such gambles are highly risky, of course, suggesting future value is dubious, not having withstood the test of time, not to mention the unpredictable mood swings in what we value from day to day. Nevertheless, a shrewd investor can hedge wisely and make a fortune on the price of tomorrow.

Understanding the relationship between time and money is essential in waking up to wealth. In the sleep state, the more we can accelerate the time between now and the dawning of our vision of endless wealth, the faster we can approach complete success. After all, the alarm clock could go off tomorrow or in the distant future, depending on when we set it and whether we choose to open our eyes when it rings.

I remember an old Alfred Hitchcock TV show. A villain had stashed the loot in the old grandfather clock, a precious antique in and of itself. A parrot kept repeating the refrain, "Time is money, look in the clock...time is money, look in the clock."

Certainly, time and money are intimately connected in our language whether we speak of living on borrowed time, investing in futures, or simply buying time. Can we buy or borrow time? Not directly, of course, but we can purchase health insurance, transplant organs, or even freeze time by embalming our bodies in ice à la Walt Disney.

We lump fame and fortune into one phrase, suggesting that wealth is both financial and temporal. The more time we can buy, the more time we have to gather more wealth. And the more wealth we gather, the more we see buying time as longevity, or even immortality. Faust was faced with the interesting dilemma of selling his soul for immortality, an indecent proposal to be sure, but what about the "six-million-dollar man" on TV? Lee Majors seemed pretty decent, if a bit not himself.

We are living longer and longer. The President no longer sends birthday cards to citizens when they reach one hundred years of age. It happens too often now. And with the baby boomers approaching senior citizenship, the percentage of the elderly population will soon be greater than ever. Longevity is something that we are looking to buy, but the cost of living is rapidly making life itself unaffordable, a cruel paradox, indeed.

As we value ourselves, so we value the world we perceive. And our value in the material world originates in the value we assign to the human body. Do we see it as a priceless work of God, something we wouldn't sell for all the money in the world? Or do we regard it as a convenient but valueless sack of flesh and bones that is in continuous and irretrievable decline? How we value the gift of physical life is the barometer of nearly all the ups and downs in the marketplace.

The concept of the biological clock is a commonly accepted metaphor. According to this image, life is limited, death is inevitable, and the longer our bodies exist in time, the quicker they are running out of time. The Grim Reaper is approaching confidently on the horizon, as we prepare for our final harvest. As Wordsworth wrote,

> Not in entire forgetfulness,
> And not in utter nakedness,
> But trailing clouds of glory do we come
> From God, who is our home;
> Heaven lies about us in our infancy!
> Shades of the prison house begin to close
> Upon the growing boy.

The view of linear life with a beginning, middle, and end affects our financial worldview as much as the previously held belief of a flat earth. Bearing the image of bodies in decay, not only do we fear the future as the ultimate end of life, we consequently fear living life fully each day, conserving our resources, our energy, our life urge. If we use up too much life today, we'll have less left to expend tomorrow. We therefore repress our feelings, creativity, and enthusiasm, subconsciously thinking that we're trapped in unsafe bodies in an unsafe universe. It's a closed system and there's no way out. Thus, we get depressed, hopeless, cynical. What's the point?

As the preacher in *Ecclesiastes* tells us, no matter how hard we work or how little, how much good we do or how much evil, how wise we become or how foolish, how righteous or how beastly:

> as the one dieth, so dieth the other; yea, they all have one breath; so that a man hath no preeminence above a beast; for all is vanity. All go unto one place; all are of the dust, and all turn to dust again.

Trapped in linear life, creeping from day to day, no wonder so many people rebel at the system. The unconscious death urge is the desire to destroy the prison of the body and return to spiritual freedom. Our addictions, unhealthy habits, and compulsive obsession with living dangerously to feel more alive or, conversely, with fitness fads, health kicks, and muscle-building are all, finally, flirtations with the dead-end goal of our own mortality.

Where is the balance between living fully and living healthfully? Is a wealthy life a long life or a rich life? And is a rich life a function of accumulated money or a succession of rich moments?

We suffer from a self-inflicted built-in obsolescence we project on most everything we perceive, experience, or construct. We build our world to destruct in time and our economic curves reflect this decadence. Our cars, fashions, music, and dance crazes go out of style almost as fast as they become popular, perhaps recycled or reincarnated twenty to thirty years later but dying rapid deaths nonetheless. We're obsessed with seeking something new to replace last year's models. Even the classics, the so-called oldies but goodies, are subject to the whims of our short-lived tastes.

Our economy flourishes on obsolescence. Our industries are testimonies to decay—the many auto repair services, waste removal companies, trend consultants, economic forecasters, and, of course, insurance and health conglomerates. Even health fads, diets, vitamins, self-help, and alternative healing techniques are victims of the law of perpetual deterioration, replaced annually by the latest, greatest trends and treatments.

How shall we ever reform our health care system in the United States until we revise our view of a healthy life? The rising cost of health is a mirror for the rising cost of living, a cost we will continue to pay until we, individually, take responsibility for handling our relationship with life and death.

Several years ago an insurance salesman visited my home. I became so angry I almost threw him out of the house. A year later, another broker came and applauded the virtues of catastrophic health insurance. The more I listened to the litany of catastrophes he predicted for me, the more depressed I became. Is this the way to build a health care system, based on pessimistic prognoses and forecasts of doom? Is this selling care, or selling fear? In China, doctors are paid to keep their patients healthy. Disease is considered an aberration of nature and, therefore, a medical failure not worthy of reward.

The darkest projection of built-in obsolescence is the doom and gloom we impose on the very planet that supports our lives. We see the future of earth through the eyes of our own mortality. We read the news and we become depressed. We look for stories of disaster, decay, decadence, and death to justify our own death wish. Then we allow our individual life urges to be subjugated to the collective secret desire for planetary catastrophe. Pessimism becomes the global Pac-Man, consuming our independent life urges one by one. Are we victims of the process of atrophy, or are we the cause? Are we lemmings sleepwalking on the dreamscape, hovering on the brink of death, thinking that the great fall will wake us up? Or can we wake up within the dream and change its outcome?

Economic cycles—personal, national, and international—are also reflective of the conflict between our life urge and death urge. When we think life is short and time is running out, it is logical to conclude that the good times can't last, money is scarce, and we can't survive in the long run. Should we spend now, living as though there's no tomorrow, or save for the future when we'll be sure to encounter hard times? Why is there never enough for both? Why do we always seem to have to sacrifice one for the other? When we express consumer confidence, our faith in the future enables us to relax, spending to increase, markets to expand. But the more we spend, the more we subconsciously trigger our fear of running out, which, in turn, stagnates the economy.

In Spain recently, I witnessed a national election. After more than a decade of economic boom following Franco's death, growth was on the decline and fear on the rise. People were losing their confidence in the future and returning to conservativism. It is so tempting to see such issues as separate from ourselves. Vote for a new party or a new president and everything will change. But nothing changes until we change our perception of ourselves as prisoners trapped in finite bodies on a finite planet in a finite universe. The window of opportunity is sealed shut, curtains drawn, until we wake up to our vision of endless wealth.

When I was in Bali, I learned that the Balinese have no past-tense or future-tense verbs in their language. At first I thought, how primitive, but the more I considered the potential of thinking in the present time, the more I began to warm up to the idea. And the more I observed what a joyful, spiritual, prosperous, co-operative, and productive people the Balinese people are, the more I became convinced that their paradise is more a state of mind than a spectacular island in the sun.

For thousands of years we have perceived the body as either a prison which houses the soul or as a temple, if we prefer the religious equivalent. We see these solid or frozen sculptures as containers in which we're trapped, our only hope is inevitable deterioration in time. So here we are, chained in limited space for a limited time. Is it punishment, karma, or the human condition? Or it is a concept we've taken for granted for so long that it's become a way of life?

According to Dr. Deepak Chopra, the truth lies beyond the

so-called facts. In his fascinating series of books and inspirational tapes which blend the richness of ancient aruyvedic healing with his training in western procedure, technology, and medicine, he paints a very startling picture of the nature of the physical universe. The human body is apparently not as solid as previously thought. In fact, it is mostly space.

If we look through a high-powered telescope into distant space, we see vast emptiness occasionally interrupted by intermittent points and clusters of stellar light. When we look through a high-powered microscope at the inner depths of the physical body, we witness a similar light show, vast and mostly empty space populated by billions of occasional molecular, atomic, and other subatomic particles. These particles are flashing rapidly throughout the body as well as in and out of the body, with no sense of solid walls and boundaries that separate the inside from the outside. So quickly do they travel, in fact, that the molecules which comprise our organs, bones, blood vessels, and tissue today are not the same molecules that were there thirteen months ago.

Moreover, these molecules are neither trapped in time nor destroyed by death. In other words, the molecules rumbling through us this year may have existed in other bodies in the past. Perhaps part of us was Oedipus, Alexander the Great, Aristotle, Copernicus, Napoleon, Queen Victoria, or Einstein. Past lives? We don't know who we were, let alone are.

In a sense, our physical bodies are nothing more than canyons of space through which invisible particles are constantly cascading. Even the molecules of our DNA are in constant flux. Then why do we perceive our bodies as being grounded in space, genetically influenced, and subject to the decaying hands of time? Good question.

We are addicted to a frozen mind-set about the body, a basic assumption that both religion and prequantum science advocated. A set mind places physical "reality" into a fixed mold and collects constant perceptual evidence to reassure its point of view. It is a projection of our ego's desire to see our bodies as separate and separating. This way we remain convinced that we are threatened by what's outside and had better trust the ego to safeguard our internal fortress. We abuse the body because we erroneously believe it to be something it is not. What we end up seeing, feeling, and experiencing is, to quote Dr. Chopra, "our skin-encapsulated egos" instead of our unlimited selves.

Our obsession with our bodies deteriorating in time parallels our view of history as the story of rise and fall, crime and punishment. The sins of the fathers are visited upon the sons. The wrongs of our past must be paid for in our future. The follies of youth give way to the pain of old age. As long as we view the future with fear sparked by guilt, death will provide both the ultimate escape and the inevitable stranglehold of this closed system called life in the body. And the body will bow subserviently to our unconscious will to destroy what encages us.

Let the buyer of old unquestioned truths beware!

As long as we peer at the universe through the preconception of finite bodies, we will see limitation everywhere, including our wallets. As we stir in our sleep and become more conscious, we can perceive the body from the standpoint of unlimited selves. The result is living based on quantum possibilities, financial, and spiritual.

Yes, as we emerge from the dream, we see that the end is the beginning and the beginning is the end, and God is truly the Alpha and the Omega. We see that the dream of birth, life, and inevitable death, of struggling hopelessly against the biological clock is the very core of our sleeping state. We recognize that things are not necessarily as they seem and that the cost of living need not be the body itself. The body is infinite and mysterious, the gift and reward we are blessed with, a vehicle for communicating love, trust, and wisdom, and for sharing our selves with the world.

We learn that the true value of life is in each holy moment; that we have the power to stop time, erase the past, forget the future, and tap into the eternal source of endless wealth, health, and well-being. *Carpe diem.* Seize the day. Not from the perspective of time running out; no, from feeling safe in the physical universe—free to go full-steam ahead every day without fear and liberated from the shackles of mind-time-space, which stagnate our motivation, creativity, and accomplishment.

Life is a continuum of ever-present glimpses into eternity. Every day we can open the window of our minds further and appreciate the view, knowing that it is only a small part of an unlimited whole, yet worthy of reverence and awe.

In the article about the 120 million-year-old weevil, the journalist mentioned the parallel to the movie *Jurassic Park* about the cloning of dinosaurs from the prehistoric DNA of a mosquito. I thought, if the movie grossed $300 million, it would add up to two and one half dollars per year for each year of the DNA's known life span. Slim pickings for dinosaur budgeting. Then, I wondered, what if the DNA of the mosquito that just stung me was retrieved in 120 million years? What if I was cloned? How much would I be worth in the year AD 120,001,993?

Chapter 21

Awaken More Each Day

W̲e'd probably all like to wake up and discover, lo and behold, our richest fantasies are dreams come true. Perhaps we're waiting for the day to dawn when, as John envisioned in Revelations, a new heaven and a new earth are born, a new Jerusalem comes down "from God out of heaven, prepared as a bride, adorned for her husband"...a day when "God shall wipe away all tears and there shall be no more death, neither sorrow, nor crying, neither shall there be any more pain."

We'd like to wake up in that new Jerusalem of pearly gates, golden streets, and walls garnished with precious stones. We'd like that moment of everlasting enlightenment, that one morning when we arise from our long sleep, our eyes permanently open to eternal health, wealth and well-being. Oh, God, wouldn't we!

In our fantasy world, that's the way it would be, an apocalyptic and permanent escape from sleep into the everlasting dream of neverneverland. One kiss from Prince Charming and we'd never need to sleep again.

Unfortunately or fortunately, depending upon how we look at it, there is a substantial difference between a vision in which time stops and heaven and earth are wed, and the unfolding of that vision within the halls of time. It takes a great deal of change to reverse the thousands of years of thinking, perceiving, feeling and experiencing the stuff of dreams. It takes the constant repetition and integration of a multitude of new habits, large and small, mental and behavioral, as well as the personal characteristics we need to develop.

It takes time to erase time. But if we take the necessary steps, one by one, individually and together, we can wake up, little by little, again and again, until finally we awaken once and for all.

The good news is that we have the choice, we have the power, and we have the time. The challenge is to choose to apply our power in each moment to the unfolding of the vision.

There are three general characteristics we need to master in order to accelerate our transformation. They are patience, persistence, and purpose. Each of these includes a variety of other qualities we acquire along the way.

It took me years to relax into patience. I would arrive early at a meeting place, wait and seethe inside, and waste much time and energy in the process. Once, when I was young, I had an appointment to meet my sister on a specific subway platform. I arrived thirty minutes early, waited two hours and left furious. I hated to be kept waiting.

Mallie taught me patience. At first I was a slow learner. (Impatient people tend to be slow learners.) I would be ready to leave the house to go on a trip while Mallie would busy herself with the last-minute details, such as making sure we had our tickets and passports, closing doors and shutting off lights, turning down the thermostats. I would pace about urgently worrying that we'd be late or miss the plane, in my little world of insufficient time. Of course, we always had more time than I realized and would arrive at the airport and inevitably have to wait. Gradually, I realized that instead of pacing and waiting and getting angry, I could do something else. I had a choice. It sounds so obvious now, but it took me many years to see that I had choice in such situations, and could use my power of choice to overcome impatience. I learned to read a book, write, meditate, or take care of last-minute details myself. Rather than spend my time waiting, I'd live my life and use my time creatively.

Patience is knowing that time is on our side. It implies both faith in the invisible and trust in what we see. Patience is a spirit of love, forgiveness, and tolerance. It is having a certainty of the outcome, and therefore not pushing, not worrying, and not projecting our hidden agendas on anyone. Patience is also being open-minded because a closed mind is an intolerant little devil that has no time for things it cannot control.

When we are patient, we are not judging every situation or person because we know that everything and everyone is sent to us for a reason. Each brings a valuable message, lesson, gift. Patience creates room to receive. Good things come to those who stretch time by being patient.

Patience is also light heartedness. When we can laugh at a situation, we lighten our loads and uplift the spirits of those around us. When we are patient, we become good listeners. We are not as eager to interrupt. We can hear beyond the words to the heart of a communication. We can hold our tongues and visions close to our chests and allow others to express themselves. We become less compulsive in our need to be right. Patience is the ability to wait for the right moment, then seize it.

Patience is spiritual seeing. When we are patient, we can observe and witness. This may seem passive but is, in fact, active, if invisibly so. When we are observing rather than reacting, we are divorcing ourselves from old thoughts, patterns, habits, and addictions by noticing them and not acting them out.

If we fall from grace from time to time, as we all do, patience is that guiltless place in which we can acknowledge our mistakes, correct them without struggle or pain, and rise again to embrace our vision.

154

Let's try to take the time to be more patient with ourselves and others each day.

I had a problem with persistence. If something did not come easily to me, I would give up. I would pretend it wasn't important and I didn't care, but I was hiding from frustration and failure. Once when I was trying to sell a screenplay I had written, I showed it to a studio executive who was quite interested. We started to talk specifics and it got very exciting. Then the negotiations stalled for a few weeks, and the combination of my impatience and lack of persistence prompted me to give the screenplay to an independent producer who never made the film. I lost much money on that one.

Persistence is the dedication of energy in a chosen direction. It requires motivation, courage, commitment, and integrity. Whereas patience asks us to trust, persistence suggests that we apply gentle pressure, navigating the course of our lives towards our destinations. We do this by planning, organizing, delegating, and making sure that jobs get done. When we sail a boat, we need the persistence to work the sails and patience to move with the wind. The more diligent we are with the sails, the more we can relax and let the wind do the work.

When persistence becomes stubbornness, it doesn't work. When we are stubborn, we grow weak, closed-minded, and heavy-handed. We are now navigating against the wind. This is struggle. When we are stubborn, we are choosing fear and are therefore threatened by differences and anything beyond our control. We become intolerant. We lose our sense of humor. Nothing is funny when we can't get our way.

When we are truly persistent, we are certain of the outcome and therefore patient and gentle in applying pressure. We are powerful, not power-hungry. We take the reins of responsibility in the driver's seat, but we do not abuse our power by forcing it upon others. When we are persistent, we do our part to guide the flow, following through to the completion of our chosen goals.

A persistent person is the captain of his or her ship. We rarely see the captain, but we know he or she is there in charge. The captain is trustworthy; delegates the workload to a competent support team; and knows where the ship is coming from, where it is now, and where it is going.

Let's try to cultivate more persistence each day, but always be willing to learn how little pressure is actually required to steer the ship.

When we have a deep sense of personal purpose, we're on track. Our purpose fuels our patience and persistence. Without purpose, we're spinning in the wind.

I remember a time in my life when I was completely unmotivated. I had no excitement, no vision, no reason for being. I'd wake up in the morning and think, "Oh no, not another day." Finally, I decided that I would not get out of bed again until I felt excited about life and knew that I had a reason for living. It took me three months. I was a total mess, unshaven and uninspired. I crawled through each day as though life was quicksand; I was sinking slowly and I didn't care. Then, one day, I awoke and everything was different. The sun was shining and I noticed the light. A breeze was blowing and I was refreshed. I was breathing and it felt good to be alive. And, more important, I knew I had purpose, a reason for being, even though I couldn't put it into words at that time. Something was guiding my life, somewhere, somehow.

I have never been bored a day since.

When we sense purpose, we're connected to our reason for being here. We are involved, engaged, and in love with life. The windows of our minds are clear. We perceive what is happening and seize every moment, opportunities appearing where obstacles once clouded our vision. When we're purposeful, our energy flows freely and our spirits soar.

We have common purpose—to love, to forgive, and to give to each other. But within that larger purpose we have our individual, personal purposes, which can be simple—to love nature, create beauty, communicate clearly, explore the planet, invent new things. When we're acting with purpose, we're usually happy, at peace with ourselves and the world. When we have a problem, we don't turn it into a conflict. We draw upon patience and persistence. We also remember our vision, which is the big picture, and our mission, which is the unfolding of our purpose.

Our purpose may contain many goals, but don't confuse the two. Our goals are our signposts, attainable in time; our purpose is our ongoing throughline which continues forever.

When we veer off track, we shouldn't judge ourselves. Who knows, we may discover something on a side road that will assist us on the freeway. When a spaceship drifts off course, those in charge don't pull their hair out and bang their heads against the wall. They simply notice the computer readings and make the appropriate adjustments. They focus on the correction, not the blame. We have the ability to apply the same objectivity to our lives, changing direction midway without damaging our vehicles.

Try to stay with purpose increasingly each day; but, when lost, seek the lessons of the wilderness, too.

When we are committed to living in a waking state more and more, our sleeping minds will compete for our attention. The ego will kick in, tempting us with the old, sleepwalking ways. We can consider this the response column to our growth.

Every action has an equal but opposite reaction. With internal transformation, planting the seed of new thought in the garden of our subconscious mind will stir up old weeds. As we entertain new beliefs about wealth, old beliefs about scarcity will rear their ugly heads. We ponder ease and pleasure; our conditioned mind replies with a chorus of struggle and pain. Remember, whatever arises is on its way out. Notice it; get out of the way. Don't get overly involved with your response column; be patient with the process and persistent with the purpose. All good visions bring up old nightmares to be healed and released.

The faster we progress, the more we may face confusion. Confusion is like going through the straits of Scylla and Charybis. The Sirens tempt us, try to steer us off course. When we are confused, we have the opportunity to welcome a new fusion occuring within us. Perhaps we can't see it. Perhaps we can only see our response column. But trust the process. Waking up to wealth is subtle. We are being stirred up, aroused from the black lagoon of our unconsciousness. The sediment of scarcity at the lower depths of our psyche is rising to the surface on its way out. Have faith!

Think of this awakening as twilight sleep. It's just before dawn and the darkest hour. We may feel hopeless at this point, not seeing any way out of the Big Sleep. Truly, we are betwixt unconsciousness and consciousness, eyes still closed, dreams abounding, but being prepared for a dawn of incomparable magnificence.

At this time, especially, it is important to immerse ourselves in the simple, daily habits, the rituals which, when repeated often enough, open our eyes to the world as we would have it be.

◆ ◆ ◆

Begin each day by taking a few deep breaths, inhaling of a new dawn and exhaling the residue of yesterday. Give thanks for the new day. Spend fifteen or twenty minutes allowing the mind to quiet down, gently focusing our attention on a mantra, thought, or affirmation without worrying if the mind drifts from time to time. You might start with a thought like, "I am unlimited wealth."

Then do physical exercise for ten to twenty minutes—yoga, nordic track, aerobics, whatever your pleasure, perhaps listening to a tape about prosperity as you work out. Rev. Ike has excellent tapes, as do Leonard Orr, Earl Nightingale, and myself.

After bathing and dressing, look in the mirror and acknowledge your assets for five minutes—the physical, mental, and spiritual qualities you most value in yourself. Then remind yourself of your purpose; re-read your vision or mission statement or a page or two from an inspirational book.

Complete the first waking hour by envisioning a good sense of how you'd like the day to be—how you want to feel, what you'd like to accomplish, and how you'd like to relate to others.

◆ ◆ ◆

We might think that we don't have the time to take an extra hour each morning for such seemingly superfluous activity. Nonsense. My experience is that when I make the time, I take the time. When I do, I have more, not less, time, energy, enthusiasm, and clarity throughout the day. And, since I'm more relaxed, I'm more patient and, thus accomplish more.

◆ ◆ ◆

If you commute to work, you can go a different way each day. Take a different route, walk on a different street, carpool, ride a different car on the train. Don't think of the commute as in between time; rather, change the scenery so it feeds your senses. That way you'll be more excited by the day.

Redecorate your office or wherever you work. Create a conscious environment that supports your commitment to wealth, health, and well-being. Hang new pictures. Get a new calendar. Find objects that symbolize wealth to remind you of your vision. Clean your desk.

As you go through the day, have the attitude that the entire day is your livelihood, not just your specific tasks. Relate to everyone, even casual encounters with strangers, with all the good will, respect, and attention you would normally reserve for important business associates. Express your gratitude and acknowledge others, even before they have earned your appreciation. The more you do this in advance, the more delighted people will be to support you. They will be empowered by your expressions of love.

Write thank you letters, notes, postcards whenever you have the time. Communicate what needs saying honestly, appropriately, responsibly. Be direct but don't blame. Ask for what you want without making others wrong. Allow others the security to give you feedback, to ask you for what they want and need. Try to be open to whatever people are trying to tell you. They need to feel that they are heard. Be a quiet listener. Be supportive. Helpful. Go the extra mile to offer assistance whenever you think of it.

If your day does not proceed as you have envisioned it, don't struggle. Setbacks happen. Let go of the stress. Take a few breaths and start over. Begin the day again in the middle. Try different approaches. Ask for help. Tell people you're having a hard day. If you lose your temper, apologize. Tell people not to take it personally. Read a few pages from an inspirational book or magazine. (Have such literature nearby at all times.) Close your eyes. Pray. Wash your face with cold water. Take a walk. Call your mother, father, mate or children. Redirect your energy any way you can.

◆ ◆ ◆

Sometimes, when I'm blocked, I write down my negative thoughts about the day so far, crumple the paper, and throw it away. It's easy, symbolic, and quickly renews me. You can also ask yourself what the lesson is you're resisting, what the gift is within the problem, or what the thought is you most need to change or remember. Or you can simply take a break. Do a crossword puzzle.

◆ ◆ ◆

Enjoy your lunch. Perhaps dine with someone you've been resisting; do some clearing. The person you've most resisted at work can often be the one who has the greatest lesson to teach you. Let it in.

Do what works. In your business and your life, remember that the repetition of a proven system is the easiest way to recreate success. Do the little tasks that you know will work. On the other hand, when you do the tasks that you keep putting off, you gain a great feeling of accomplishment. Make the phone calls you've been avoiding, communicate to the person you most need to speak to, and reach out to someone who might be avoiding you.

At day's end, acknowledge others and their efforts. Thank them for being in your life. (If you forget to do this, do it in your mind.) Complete any unresolved communication. Review what you've accomplished during the day. List the successes you've had, major or minor. Then list the lessons you've learned, what you would do differently next time. Clarify what sort of day you want tomorrow. Take a few breaths again and let the day go. Trust that now you're more awake to the wealth that surrounds you than you were twenty-four hours ago.

When you go to bed, remember this—you may sleep, you may dream, you may sleepwalk through many more nights and days. But a giant who knows he or she sleeps, who understands the nature of the dreamscape, and who awakens more each day is a financial giant on the horizon.

◆ ◆ ◆

Chapter 22

The Return of
the Sleeping Giant

As long as the Radiant Child lay in the cave, everything went well for the villagers. After all, they were financial giants now, enjoying their enormous wealth and commonwealth. At first, they celebrated life twenty-four hours a day, but when they were tired of parties they returned to work. The village rapidly became a beehive of activity.

Each person worked at what he or she loved most. They became a community of artists, craftsmen, and builders. The dancers danced, the singers sang, and the musicians made exquisite, celestial music, heard on the hills for miles around. The carvers carved, the glassblowers blew glass, and the builders built. Indeed, there was much construction everywhere as, one by one, all the little houses were transformed into huge dwellings suitable for giants.

Each villager enjoyed the others' creations, everyone contributing their excellence to the quality of life in the village. The doctors no longer needed to tend to the sick but, rather, assisted the healthy to stay well. The lawyers, judges, and politicians, together with the priests, devoted their time to writing a new town charter based on the principles of commonwealth. Even the philosophers, who previously had argued amongst themselves about most everything, now theorized peacefully about the nature of the universe. All agreed that life was good, wealth was endless, and the village was a promised land of dreams come true.

The villagers were remarkably healthy, strong, and youthful. They smiled and frequently could be seen shaking hands, embracing one another, and patting each other's back. Their good nature overflowed in these spontaneous expressions of love.

If strangers arrived in town, the giant villagers would invite their little guests for a feast, and offer them the best bed in town for the night. If they were poor, they would be offered gifts of gold before they departed the next morning.

The children were highly regarded. After all, they had saved the village. Giants themselves, they invented new games, such as cloud-puffing, lake-hopping, and mountain-jumping. Their education became a matter of fine-tuning their prolific abilities.

At first, the children visited the cave every day, playing with the Radiant Child and taking care of Him, though He hardly seemed to need it. Nevertheless, they would bathe Him, feed Him, and dress Him up. Sometimes, they would lift Him and toss Him gently around like a beachball. The Radiant Child delighted in the attention and blessed the giant children with laser beams of light that zoomed out of His hands.

The villagers abounded in such endless wealth that they never even visited the cave to retrieve their treasure. At first, they would go to the cave to make sure their treasure was secure and to see the Radiant Child, but they never took their wealth out of the cave. They didn't need it. They exchanged goods and services, giving freely to one another, and never thinking about anything in return. They lived one day at a time and no longer marked time. Everything was now. Nobody got older or ill or depressed or bored. Nor did they worry about the future or regret the past. No one gave these matters much thought any more.

And so life flourished for what seemed like an eternity.

The new village charter had proclaimed the Valley of the Sleeping Giant and the Cave of the Radiant Child holy sites. As with most holy sites, after a while only the tourists visited them. The villagers were all too preoccupied with their giant happiness to be curious about the Radiant Child. Even the giant children gradually stopped visiting the cave.

One morning the philosophers awoke and decided to discuss a new topic: Why was the village so happy? They didn't argue. They didn't disagree or debate. They merely wondered in unison. Soon their curiosity became a focus for the other villagers. Nobody could answer the simple question, though many had theories. One said that they were a test case for the whole world. Nah, said the others. Another suggested that they deserved their happiness because they had suffered so much in the past. Nah, said the others. A third said they were just lucky. Everybody laughed.

The next day, one of the children, the girl who had been so instrumental in awakening the Giant, decided to visit the cave and ask the Radiant Child the question. She and several friends tiptoed over the hillside, trying not to be noticed or create a disturbance. When they arrived at the cave of endless wealth, it was very quiet. The girl entered the cave, which was filled with glittering gold and gemstones, but there was no sign of the Radiant Child. The children searched the vicinity, thinking that the Child was somewhere in the area, but there was no sign of Him anywhere. They returned to the village but didn't mention the disappearance. They went back to the cave the next morning and every morning for seven days, but it was always the same, no Radiant Child.

Gradually, word spread that the Radiant Child had vanished. At first, there was much interest in His possible whereabouts, this replacing the question of the villages' happiness as the principle topic of conversation. Some of the villagers began to worry about the Child. Some felt guilty that they hadn't paid more attention to Him. Others wondered if they had done something wrong and would be punished. Most, however, continued about their business cheerfully and soon village life returned to its normal, blissful state.

But the seeds of unrest had been planted.

One morning everything changed. It was a cold and windy day. As the villagers awoke, they sensed that something was different, but nobody could decide what it was. The reason they could not determine the problem was that they could not remember it.

They had forgotten they were giants.

Slowly, almost imperceptibly at first, the behavior of the villagers began to change. The singers sang less frequently, the dancers rarely danced, and the musicians lay down their instruments. The painters stopped painting, the sculptors stopped sculpting, and the carvers lay down their tools.

Like a dark cloud approaching from over the mountains, the shadow of fear was once again cast upon the village, hiding the light of love that had previously enveloped it. Smiles gave way to frowns and good will to ill will. No longer were the villagers thanking each other, shaking hands, embracing, or patting each other's backs. Nor were they generous of spirit, pondering more and more how much they could get for what they gave. Suspicion, anger, and resentment gripped their souls. Peace gave way to conflict, and struggle replaced ease and pleasure.

The philosophers debated and quarreled amongst themselves, and the children were disciplined and punished whenever they spoke up and asked their parents why they were behaving so strangely.

The builders wanted to build something to raise the spirit of the village again, something that would bring everyone together one more time. They decided to construct a grand tower with a clock on top—a glockenspiel—at the center of the village square. At first, there was much excitement and everyone joined in the effort. It seemed as if the village was reliving its happier days.

But as the tower rose higher and higher, people questioned

its purpose and value and argued about its design. Many thought it a waste of time, money, and energy to erect such a colossal structure. Gradually, two factions emerged, one which wanted to complete the tower and the other which wanted to tear it down. They called themselves the Constructionists and Destructionists respectively. There was a great deal of bitter debate between the two parties. The Destructionists resorted to sabotage and terrorism to halt the efforts of the Constructionists, who retaliated by forming an armed police force and building a new courthouse and prison. (The old ones had been converted to an art gallery and theatre.)

In a short time the village was transformed from heaven to hell and work on the glockenspiel ground to a halt. Then the villagers made another monumental decision. They decided to take their treasure from the cave and divide it equally among the citizens of the village. When they did this, they were amazed to discover that the divided wealth did not give each villager very much at all. They couldn't understand why this was so and began to spread rumors about thieves and looters from neighboring villages. And so, they built a great wall around the entire village with only four entrances, guarded twenty-four hours a day.

Strangers were no longer welcome.

Poverty and hard times descended upon the villagers. Trade diminished and tourism disappeared due to their mistrust of their neighbors. The marketplace was decimated by dishonesty, swindling and, finally, a reluctance to exchange anything. Sullen and morose, the villagers' work deteriorated. They became sloppy, lazy and dirty. They didn't care any more. Soon, the village looked like a city slum.

By this time the children were fed up with their parents' behavior. Led by the young girl, they once again planned to sneak out of the village and search for the long-lost Radiant Child, whom they were convinced was actually the Sleeping Giant. They packed food and supplies and waited for the full moon to guide them.

One night, when the elders were asleep and the guards at the gates had finally dozed off, the children divided into four groups and tiptoed in silence out of the village to the countryside. Each group, they had agreed, would search the hills and valleys north, south, east, and west for one month, then return to the village. They embarked upon their mission filled with hope and the spirit of adventure.

When the elders awoke and saw that the children were gone, they immediately forgot about fighting amongst themselves and huddled together out of guilt and fear. For no matter how low they had descended on the ladder of human behavior, they still loved their children and felt remorseful about how poorly they had treated them. Some of the elders ventured outside the village walls and cried out their children's names. Others visited the now empty cave, thinking their children would be there. When asked for advice, the philosophers and priests could think of nothing to say.

Meanwhile, the four tribes of children plodded on, each in the chosen direction. They avoided neighboring villages because they knew there was great animosity between their village and others. Each tribe climbed higher and higher into the mountains, unsure of where they were going but guided as if by an unseen hand.

When the first tribe climbed to the top of the tallest mountain east, they sat down to rest, exhausted from their journey. They had eaten almost all of their food and were hungry. Since there was not enough food to go around, they decided to save what little they had. The sun was rising over a distant mountain and the children bathed in the warm rays of a new day. Suddenly, they saw a stranger walking towards them. He was a very old man with a long, white beard and a cane. An old, fat pig followed him.

The leader of the tribe of children rose to greet the old man.

"Hello, fellow traveler. Where are you going?"
"Hello, young man. I am walking my pig."
"I wonder if you can help us. We are looking for a Radiant

Child who once was a Sleeping Giant." The stranger scratched his beard, as if trying to remember something. He asked why they wanted to find this child who was a giant, and they told him of the plight of their village.

"So," the old man finally said, "it is very important that you find your Radiant Child!"

"We'd give anything."

"Hmm. In that case, do you have any food?"

"Well, actually, only a few slices of bread and cheese, and we have a long journey home."

"Give me your food," the stranger said, not in a demanding way, but, nonetheless, in a tone that could not be refused. The children gave the stranger their remaining food. As soon as he received it, he turned, bent down, and fed the food to his old pig, whereupon they both vanished into thin air.

Back in the village, the elders arose from their doldrums and decided to complete their tower and glockenspiel. They reasoned that it would keep them busy and when it was finished, its huge bells would ring throughout the countryside. Perhaps the children would answer the call and return home. So, once again, the village became a beehive of activity. Although they were sad, guilty, and terribly worried about their children, the villagers slowly rekindled the spirit of kindness and cooperation amongst themselves.

The second and third tribes of children had similar experiences to the first tribe. One went to the highest mountain in the southern region and stopped to rest on the summit, whereupon an old man appeared, followed by a camel. When the children told the old man their story, he asked for their water, which had almost run out. Nevertheless, they gave him what was left, which he in turn allowed his camel to drink, both then vanishing from sight.

The third tribe headed to the northernmost mountain. It was

very cold when they reached the top. The children wrapped themselves in blankets, lit a fire, and shivered in despair. Again, an old man appeared, this time with a herd of sheep in tow. He asked the children for their blankets in payment for information about the Radiant Child. When the children handed the stranger their woolen blankets, he calmly covered each and every sheep with one, whereupon he and his herd disappeared.

The fourth tribe was led by the famous young girl. They climbed the westernmost peak and collapsed from exhaustion as the sun was setting. No stranger appeared. No pig, no camel, no sheep, nothing. The next morning they headed down the mountain, utterly hopeless and defeated.

There was a stir of excitement in the village square. The villagers gathered by the grand tower and looked up at the clock. The sun was about to rise and the glockenspiel was ready for its first performance. At precisely sunrise, the clock chimed its beatific bells, its elaborate machinery was set in motion. The chimes played a romantic waltz. Suddenly, the doors beneath the clock opened, and a parade of twirling, painted mechanical ballerinas and knights on white horses danced majestically in circles round and round their stage. The villagers cheered wildly, throwing their hats into the air, celebrating their exquisite creation.

In fifteen minutes the show was finished and would not be repeated until sunset. The villagers waited expectantly, hoping their children would respond to the cavernous chimes. But nothing happened.

Several days later, three of the four tribes returned from their sojourns. Though empty-handed, the children were delighted to find their parents in good spirits again, and the elders rejoiced in the return of their children. The children marvelled at the glockenspiel and there was much celebration and festivity. However, the fourth tribe of children had not yet returned.

A storm was brewing—lightning, thunder, torrential rains. The fourth tribe was trudging slowly down the mountainside.

The children were cold, wet, and shivering, but that was the least of their worries. They had failed in their mission. All was lost. The young girl who led them was crestfallen; tears mixed with raindrops on her rosy cheeks.

Finally, as they approached the Valley of the Sleeping Giant, they could go no further. Though only a few hours from their village, they had to stop and rest. And so, the young girl led her tribe into the cave for shelter from the storm. It was empty.

They huddled together in an attempt to keep warm, but it was useless. They were sneezing, sniffling, and coughing. Suddenly, an old man with a long, white beard and a cane entered the cave. He was followed by a herd of twelve pigs, twelve camels, and twelve sheep. When he and his entourage arrived, the children clung together in one giant shiver.

The cave was very crowded. The animals stood patiently in the pouring rain outside the entrance. Finally, the young girl rose and asked the old man where he was going.

"I am looking for a dry place to spend the night with my little friends," he replied, a twinkle in his eye.

The girl looked around at her fellow travelers. They were a ragged group. She knew they would not want to surrender the cave to this old man and his animals. But she also knew that they would follow her leadership. It was almost dusk and the countryside was gloomy.

"You can have this cave," she said finally.

"This will do," said the old man, motioning for his herd to enter the cave, lie down and rest, as the children rose and began to leave. "You are very kind," he added whereupon he took out a sack filled with bread, cheese, water, and blankets and proceeded to offer his goods to the children.

"Thank you," the girl said, "but why don't you keep your food and your blankets. You need them more than we do. Our village is a short way from here, and we can get what we need there."

"You are very kind," repeated the old man. Suddenly, the children heard a loud noise. It was the glockenspiel announcing day's end. They bid the old man and his animals good night and hurried across the valley towards home.

When they arrived, the entire village cheered and hugged and breathed one collective sigh of relief. The storm rapidly abated, and they looked to the west where they could see the brilliant red, yellow, orange, and lavender rays of sunshine streaking across the heavens.

The next morning the young girl awoke at dawn. She heard the waltz of the glockenspiel. Otherwise, there was no sound. Everyone had slept late. She dressed and went outside. Everything was aglitter. At first, she thought it was the dew, but when she looked closer, she feasted her eyes. The village had been miraculously transformed into a kingdom of unparalleled richness, streets lined with gold, walls made of gemstones, and gates glistening with white pearl. Every building was strewn with crystals, emeralds, diamonds, and sapphires.

Amazed, she walked out to the Valley of the Sleeping Giant. It was a warm, sunny day; birds were singing and a gentle breeze whistled through the trees. She looked everywhere, but there was no sign of the Giant. She approached the cave. It was quiet. Not wanting to disturb the old man and his animals, she was about to leave when she saw from the corner of her eye a golden glow emanating from the cave.

She entered the cave. It was empty, yet seemed filled with a shimmering golden fairy dust. There was no sign of either the old man or his animals. Although there was no treasure, the magnificent glow seemed even more precious. She looked for the Radiant Child, thinking He must be somewhere, but there was no trace of Him, other than the Radiance itself. Suddenly, she saw a piece of paper, a note, which she read.

"Thank you," it said. "You are very kind. You no longer need me."

♦ *Chapter 23* ♦

The Great
Reawakening

To wake up to wealth is to reawaken to wealth. To recognize wealth is to know it again. Each time we know it, we become more familiar with it. At first wealth might seem like a stranger, then an acquaintance, then a friend, and then a constant companion. Finally it becomes a natural part of who we are.

It is always far easier to make our second or third million dollars, should we have the misfortune of mismanaging our first or second. At least we know we made it once. We know we can do it, and within us is the knowledge required to do it again.

If we have not yet made our first million, perhaps we've made our first $100,000 or $10,000. The same principle holds true. The only difference is the number of zeroes.

When we calculate all the income we've received in our lives, we see a surprisingly large sum. We can easily make that again in a much shorter time. How short depends upon how quickly we reawaken to wealth.

The story of the Sleeping Giant takes us through seven stages on the journey to wealth. At first, the villagers are financially secure, their wealth stored in the cave of the commonwealth. This is Stage One, which we can think of as our prenatal reality of wealth, our preparation for our final awakening later. We have everything we need. The cave is like the womb—warm, radiant, supporting, nurturing. If we never had the experience of being connected to an abundant and loving universe in the womb, we'd never know that it was our birthright. We wouldn't anticipate it, search the world for it, and recognize it when we found it.

In Stage Two, the villagers sleep. They become sleeping financial giants. They sleepwalk through the dreamscape of struggle and scarcity, forgetting that the cave is still within reach. Thus, a Sleeping Giant appears, reflecting this condition. Unfortunately, the villagers misinterpret the Giant and allow Him to come between them and the cave.

In this stage, the Giant is like the obstetrician who delivers us but, in so doing, separates us from the womb, from mother. We are born into a world of attack and conflict. We must leave the warmth and nourishment of the womb behind. We cry often, missing the all-pervasive sense of well-being we once knew. We sleep. We cling to our mother's breast, trying to fill the emptiness we feel. We hunger for nourishment, love, wealth.

Of course, we must be born. We must emerge from the cave to live in the light. We must shed our dependencies and codependencies, and learn that when cords are cut we are liberated as well as separated.

In Stage Three, the children rescue the village, waking up the gentle Giant. At this point, everyone is transformed into financial giants themselves and the Sleeping Giant becomes a Radiant Child. This is analogous to the Christ child, come to bridge the gap between heaven and earth and unite us in a golden age.

As children, we recover quickly from the trauma of birth—the loss and separation—returning once again to the promised land of love, wealth, and well-being. We are once again provided for and prosperous; time—past and future—have little meaning for us. We play in the land of milk and honey.

In Stage Four, the villagers suddenly became self-conscious. They ask themselves why they are so happy. Once they question their condition, they lose their innocence. They become skeptical. And so, the Radiant Child disappears.

The village gradually falls from grace. The villagers divide the wealth and discover that their individual portions are meager. (Of course, when we separate from the whole, we reduce our share.) They quarrel. They reprimand the children. They start building a veritable Tower of Babel with a clock to announce the passage of time, whereas, previously they lived in timeless bliss. They struggle. They form two opposing factions, one creative, the other destructive. They fear the outside world and thus build a great wall.

As we grow older, we learn from our elders, whom we respect and believe, that reality is not what we thought it was in our youth. We're told to wake up from our dreams, take a good look at reality, and prepare ourselves for the pain and suffering of adulthood. Go to school. Learn a trade. Become a professional. Life is a rat race. Only the fit survive. We leave our childlike innocence, our timeless dream of endless wealth, and live in the reality our elders have created. After all, they should know the truth. They're older and supposedly wiser. They've already gone through their rites of passage. At this stage, we place our elders on pedestals, substitutes for our own inner knowledge.

We forget. We fall asleep once again in the name of waking up. We gather evidence to support our elder's view, not our own. We read the newspapers and magazines, watch TV and films and soon we are sleepwalking through the same dreamscape as they are. We don't like it, but what can we do? It's the "human condition."

Many of us live this reality for a very long time.

In Stage Five, the children embark upon their vision quest. They can no longer tolerate their parents' misery. They become prodigal sons and daughters, exploring the four corners of the earth in search of the long-lost secret of the Sleeping Giant. Now they go through their initiation rites, tested by the mysterious stranger who asks them to give what they cannot afford—their last food, water, blankets, shelter. The children give wholeheartedly. When the stranger passes these precious goods to the animals who seem to least need them, he is teaching the children a valuable lesson—when we give what we think we need, we demonstrate our freedom from scarcity. We can now wake up to wealth.

The children pass their test. They prove they are patient, persistent, purposeful, and generous. They have sown the seeds for the reawakening of the village.

In Stage Six, the elders, missing their children, begin their reawakening. They stop fighting. They huddle together. They pray. They return to right livelihood, building their tower from a spirit of cooperation, not conflict. They construct a glockenspiel—graceful, beautiful and musically charming. The clock is no longer a monument to the inevitable passage of time but, rather, a testimony to the healing hands of time, as well as the creation of community based on love-in-action.

At this stage, the spirit of commonwealth is reborn which, incidentally, coincides with the moment of generosity displayed by the children.

Stage Seven is the final awakening, the return to endless wealth. The prodigal sons and daughters return home. The glockenspiel performs its magical tale of twirling ballerinas and knights on white horses, female and male power dancing in unison.

When the young girl awakens the following morning, the streets are lined with gold, the walls are ablaze with precious gemstones, the gates are glowing with white pearls and the buildings sparkle with jewels. A new Jerusalem has come to earth.

The final reawakening has transpired. The village has internalized its wealth. The Sleeping Giant and the Radiant Child have transformed from external symbols to internal qualities.

All is well.

The Price of Freedom

The best things in life are free we're told. But we also know that the price of many items we need, want, and value is escalating rapidly year after year. Like the national debt, personal expenses seem out of control, skyrocketing with a will of their own, making it more and more difficult for us to climb the mountain to financial independence.

There is one thing we treasure, the price of which remains forever the same. Freedom. Understanding the nature of freedom, its costs and rewards, can help accelerate our waking up to wealth.

Certainly, we love to be free. And we love to receive things at no cost. But we always pay a price for anything of value in life, whether it be in dollars or energy. Without giving, there can be no receiving. Even those who win the lottery pay a price for their sudden wealth, often reporting great emotional or psychological upheaval as a result of their winnings. Value is only experienced in exchange. On some level, everything costs something, even freedom.

When we are children, testing our boundaries and independence, we think that when we are older we will finally be free. We equate freedom with the ability to control our lives and not having to take orders. However, when we are adults, we discover that the freedom we anticipated is as elusive as a butterfly.

We think that wealth is freedom. If only we had enough money, we reason, we would be free of the burdens and worries that shackle us. Of course, this is not true. We might accumulate great financial wealth and yet suffer pain and disease, relationship problems, anxiety, depression, and despair. Our cash flow might be healthier than our life flow.

What is financial freedom? Is it having enough wealth so that we don't have to work for a living? Is it having our money do the work by earning the interest and dividends we can live on? These might be our financial goals, and we would be happier if we were to attain them. But financial freedom is more the ability to free ourselves from our dysfunctional relationship with money.

The more we can divorce our financial life from the emotional and psychological baggage we bring to it, the more free we feel, money or no money. The more we are dependent upon money, the more we are victims of it and, therefore, the more we need it in order to feel happy. When we can detach our emotional needs from our cash flow, we are free to practice money-mastery.

We frequently look for satisfaction in the wrong places. Instead of meeting our emotional, psychological, and spiritual needs in our relationships, we try to accumulate money. Yet money cannot buy love, which deeply nourishes us and heals our empty hearts. We can only be fulfilled from the inside out, yet, in our ignorance, we are addicted to possession as a false substitute for wholeness.

We want to be provided for, supported. Since we are no longer children who can expect our parents to do the job, we transfer our neediness to money, now giving it the power over us. Many of us become slaves to money, whether we have much or little.

We might ask ourselves, are we working for money or is money working for us? Our answer will reveal our basic financial relationship. If it's the former, then money is our boss. If it's the latter, then we're in control.

Janice Joplin sang that "freedom's just another word for nothing left to lose." Many people in the newly independent republics of eastern Europe might agree with her. As miserable as they were living under totalitarian regimes, many complain that the situation is worse now. At least communism provided for their basic needs. Freedom, for these people, is equivalent to chaos, poverty, and hunger.

Recently I was in Germany, a prosperous nation to be sure. Now, with thirty million new citizens from the eastern sector, plus millions of other immigrants, the burden of prosperity is creating bitterness. What I heard was a typical family story. One sibling labors to support the family unit; the other is accustomed to being taken care of. Resentment is the inevitable result.

Consider the millions of people who suddenly discovered themselves living in a free market system. Political freedom is what we supposedly want. Yet the privilege of living in a free nation implies the challenge to overcome fear as well as the opportunity to create freely. When people are conditioned to work for the state, they can become robotic cogs in the wheel, unthinking participants in the bureaucratic machinery. When the system is suddenly dismantled, the wheel grinds to a screeching halt. The people-parts of the machine, suddenly liberated from their familiar roles, are now forced to stand on their own two feet. And the road ahead seems strange, unfriendly, even threatening.

It's not easy for a cog to reinvent the wheel.

The German philosopher Schopenhauer suggested that freedom was an illusion. He believed that we are like stones thrown into the air, imagining, midflight that we control our destination but, in reality, are governed by natural laws defining our projectiles. Is that true? I don't think so. We are more likely pilots of the spacecraft that can correct our flight plan as we journey through the universe. Yes, we are affected by forces beyond our control, but we do have the ability to direct our lives by our free will, intelligence, and imagination.

We cherish freedom, yet we don't always make the most of it. When we don't use it, we lose it. Many Americans, living in arguably the freest country on earth, act as though we are imprisoned by forces we cannot influence. We wave our freedom like a flag in the wind, but when it comes to thinking freely, let alone choosing freely, we seem incapable of the effort required. Jean Genet, on the other hand, sat in a prison cell writing brilliant plays. Mahatma Gandhi and Martin Luther King gladly marched to jail to demonstrate their freedom in action.

Who is free, the person who is born free or the one who thinks and acts freely?

When I question people on their attitude toward freedom, many express a basic resentment. Although they treasure their freedom, they feel it is a burden. They say that if there was a God, He would have created a perfect universe and they wouldn't have to make such difficult choices in their lives. Moreover, they point to the pain, poverty, and suffering in the world as excuses for their own misery. These are free people who wouldn't sell their freedom at any price, complaining about the results of freedom.

It seems to me that in a perfect universe, the Creator would allow His creation to participate freely in the evolution of His purpose. So it is. We have the choice to create or destroy, love or hate, as well as to gather abundance or scarcity, make peace or war. We can live as one family on one planet or as separate and isolated islands. The power of decision is ours. Yours, everyone's.

There is only one price we must pay for our freedom and that is responsibility. We often haggle at the cost.

Responsibility, according to some, means the ability to respond. Some say it is the willingness to sponsor one's actions. I like both these ideas. When we are responsible, we are "owning" the fact that we can freely choose our own responses. We don't have to be reactive to the people and situations that life sends us. And we can stand behind our actions, backing them up, and living and learning from the consequences.

We are responsible because we are creative. We create by choosing what we believe, what we value, and what we want, and then demonstrating our choice in our actions. Our lives are works of art and we are the artists. If we don't like the way life is turning out, we can change it or start over. But we are the ones who must initiate creation.

"God helps those who help themselves," my mother always said. When we choose to align ourselves with the intelligent and purposeful direction of the universe, we naturally live in harmony, peace, and prosperity. When we choose to disassociate from the unity of life, we face the results of such decisions. And each day we live to choose again.

When we hear the word "responsibility," we yawn. It's boring and exhausting. We mistake responsibility for obligation, guilt, and emotional debt, thinking it entails doing what we don't want to do but were told we should do. This is erroneous thinking.

To be responsible is to be guiltless, to know that we are the innocent creators of the results in our lives, financial or otherwise. When we reside in the realm of guiltlessness, we can feel the excitement of responsibility, the creative freedom it implies. We can be children again.

My granddaughter is four years old. The other day she was playing in the swimming pool with her father. She was splashing him and having fun. So was he. Then he told her to stop splashing him, but she continued. When she wouldn't stop, he told her to get out of the pool. She sat down beside me in tears. He came to the edge of the pool and asked her if she knew why she was being punished. He told her that if she knew why and apologized, she could get back into the pool. She thought for a moment and then answered that it was because she splashed him. She said she was sorry. He replied, no, that wasn't it. She searched for the right answer. Finally, he told her that it was because she didn't listen to him when he told her to stop splashing.

She got back into the pool. Within a minute she was busy splashing him again, soon to be sent into exile one more time. In her mind, she was guiltless for splashing him. He had even told her that was not the problem. When he asked her to stop again, she couldn't understand because in her mind splashing was okay.

She was guiltless, free, and trying to learn responsibility. But it can be complicated to comprehend what we're doing, let alone thinking, that is creating the unwanted consequence. We need to listen quietly to ourselves as well as to the feedback we receive from our actions. The latter can be a clue to the former since the causative factors within us are often buried in layers of the subconscious material.

When we listen quietly, we meditate. The ripples of our surface thoughts settle down. We can then dive deeper into the sea of consciousness. When we do so, we attain a new kind of freedom, a true freedom. We transcend our egos.

In a sense, we are prisoners of our egos. And the tyranny of a little mind is probably the greatest oppression we can suffer. It is painful to be abused by the tyranny of other people's minds. But it is far worse to be beleaguered by hordes of negative thoughts from our own minds. Until we take responsibility for choosing to transcend our limited thinking, we will be continuously assaulted by limited results.

We are free. We are responsible. We are innocent. And we have the power to alter our thinking, behavior, and therefore our experiences. We can choose new actions, reactions, and interactions with all of life and, in so doing, release ourselves from the inner chains that bind us.

We are the Sleeping Giants. We are the Radiant Children.

Whenever we open our eyes, we have the opportunity to see a new universe. Whenever we take a breath, we can access new inspiration.

The world is a magnificent garden. And we have the tools we need to cultivate a rich harvest which, in turn, blesses all humanity.

May we all use our tools well, thank God for His guidance, live long and prosper.

How This Book Came to Be

When I was a child, I thought I was rich. I always had everything I needed and most everything I wanted as well. Mom said I had expensive taste, but I never saw this as a problem. Dad was a lawyer and owned several buildings. Every first Sunday of the month he'd go down to the Lower Eastside to collect rent. He'd come home with what seemed like an enormous amount of money, sit at the kitchen table, and count it. I'd sit there opposite him, my elbows resting on the table, my head in my hands, eyes opened wide, taking in the abundance. We were rich.

We must all begin life with a feeling of abundance. In the womb, we float in a bubble. All our needs are met and we don't ever have to earn a living. Our only job is to be and grow, and literally live in the lap of luxury. Could this be a cruel cosmic joke, the calm before the storm, or the product of a twisted imagination, that life is so easy before we enter a world seemingly so difficult? Or is it, as I believe, that the peace and bliss of the prenatal condition is preparation for what is to come—the promised land—a place to relax and feel supported, a rehearsal for what is our birthright on this planet?

As I grew older, my eyes opened wider and I began to see "reality." We lived in Brooklyn in a middle class neighborhood, Flatbush. We had a two-bedroom apartment in a six-story building. Some of my friends had more money than I did, some less. I remember negotiating a raise in my allowance from three to five dollars a week, which was about average among my peers. I remember some of the neighbors having bigger or better TVs or cars, and vacations that we couldn't afford. Not that I suffered from my apparent lack. We'd rent a bungalow in the Catskills for the summer, or drive to Cape Cod in New England, or even Quebec for two-week holidays. Once my dad took me to Miami for a week—just the two of us. Some of my friends never went anywhere.

I remember learning that some people were "really" rich. There was one family in the jewelry business that lived in a huge house several blocks away. I'd walk by what seemed like a mansion and wonder what it would be like to live in such a big house, for the first time feeling excluded from true wealth. Then there were times my parents would talk about my dad's business partner, Sol, who lived in Scarsdale. Every time I'd hear the name Scarsdale, images of mink coats and Cadillacs would spin in my head. And there were days we'd drive up Park Avenue, where the buildings were lined with doormen and limousines.

When I was thirteen, my parents sent me to summer camp in the mountains of North Carolina. There were kids there from everywhere and many of them talked about wealth I had never even seen. Ranches and horses, sailboats and yachts, skiing in Switzerland, fancy prep schools—the dancing images in my mind would keep me awake nights. I fell in love with a girl who lived on Long Island. After the summer I visited her on weekends. Her dad was an architect who had designed their magnificent contemporary house, equipped with skylights and sliding glass doors, redwood paneling, and a huge kitchen with a free-standing counter. Even a big oak tree grew in from the middle of the house and through the roof. Then there was the yacht and the times I was allowed to take the helm.

However, at the same time that my expensive taste was being fed, I was learning my financial limitations.

My mom would take me clothes shopping. I'd always want something we couldn't afford. She'd drag me to the bargain basement and buy me things I didn't really like. I'd beg her for the one shirt or jacket I did want. Sometimes she'd give in, but not without reminding me, "Money doesn't grow on trees, you know."

Little by little, I was learning that I was separate from the abundance that surrounded me. I was becoming financially educated. I began to think about what I would do when I grew up, whether I'd be rich or poor. These were the fifties and I was in public high school. My mom asked me if I wanted to go to a private school, and I remember feeling confused. On the one hand, money didn't grow on trees and we shopped in bargain basements; on the other hand, here she was offering me an expensive private school. I said no. I didn't want to be any more of a burden than I already was.

I was groomed to be a doctor or a scientist, my sister a writer. I don't know why we were expected to do this, but these thoughts were clearly in the air at that time for boys and girls. So, I did well in my science classes and my sister did well in English. The only trouble was that I liked to paint and write. I was happiest when I was being creative. I could see my father struggling with his career. He had wanted to be an actor, I learned, but it was just after the Depression and his dad had insisted on a more practical career. I decided that I would do what I wanted for a living, but I had no idea what that was. Suddenly, it was time to apply to colleges.

My sister had gone to Barnard and I wanted to follow in her footsteps at Columbia. My mom was supportive, but my dad was feeling the financial crunch. He insisted that I go to Brooklyn College, a free city school, unless I was committed to becoming a doctor. His reasoning was that if I were headed towards medical school, a degree from Columbia would be a good investment, but that if I were going to study liberal arts, I might as well go to Brooklyn College. Weighing all my options, I said I'd be a doctor and enrolled at Columbia, knowing full well I had lied to my father.

Not that I had a free ride. I took out student loans, worked part-time, and lived in a tenement on the Lower East Side, near my father's rapidly deteriorating real estate investments. These were years of financial irony. On the one hand, I was at an ivy league school surrounded by great wealth. Columbia owned some of the most valuable real estate in New York—a stark contrast to dad—and many of the students were either born rich or their children would be. On the other hand, I lived in near-poverty, climbing five floors to my roach-infested, railroad flat several times a day.

I was financially split: my dad's voice and common sense pulled me toward a career in medicine, while my heart tugged me in different directions. I grew more and more interested in writing and theatre, my dad's unrealized dream. I majored in dramatic literature but told no one. I remember my advisor summoning me to his office at the end of junior year, reviewing my records, and telling me that I was going to have difficulty completing my pre-med requirements before graduation. When I mentioned that I had switched my major without notifying him, he just laughed.

The sixties were a time of great financial confusion for me. I was swept up in the spirit of rebellion, rejected all authority but claimed none of my own. I made no distinction between politics and economic traditions. The values of my parents' generation were suddenly valueless, the American dream now a "bum trip." When my mom asked me what I was going to do with my life, I told her not to worry, I'd be a millionaire by my thirtieth birthday.

Maybe I expected a financial windfall in reward for my resistance and righteousness. Maybe I was just trying to get her off my back.

Still, when you're born on neither side of the tracks, you tend to ride the train you're on. At least, I did. I married the daughter of a wealthy New York surgeon, spent weekends at the proverbial house in the Hamptons, and received my masters degree in dramatic literature from Columbia. The unrest in me was stirring as never before, and my future was blowing in the wind.

I then went to Yale Drama School where I received a scholarship, still thinking that I could have the best of both worlds, my creative self-fulfillment and a million dollars by my thirtieth birthday. At Yale, however, the split hit the fan. By this time Vietnam had become America's living hell. And drugs had become the expression of my generation's desire to alter its mind. Kennedy and King were dead. The Beatles, Stones, and Dead were alive. So the counter-culture became my trip, rebellion my vehicle, and financial well-being a fading dream. I burned my draft card, organized protests against the war and for civil rights, and almost forgot that I was in school.

My marriage turned into another institution I rebelled against. At that time a college campus was a huge theatre for the psychodrama of an explosive generation. I remember when The Living Theatre came to Yale, mixing stunning drama with street politics, and, like a pop Pied Piper, led so many of us into the emotional wilderness of our souls.

I dropped out of Yale and marriage, secluding myself in a country house that one of my radical professors provided for his wayward students. When I took stock of my life, I realized that I had now turned a corner. There was no going back. So, I took off for London and started TNT, The New Theatre, and worked with British actors interested in American improvisation. Money was scarce. I lived on a writing award I had won at Yale, and the few pounds I could earn here and there. But I was happier than I had been in years and, for the first time, I felt that there was a force guiding me that might even love me. I didn't spend a great deal of time thinking about this force, but I experienced a definite shift in my relationship with the universe. Where there had been chaos and confusion, there was now a new-found faith in the future that I could not deny.

My financial evolution was shifting into a new phase. I had passed through my childhood illusion that I was born wealthy. And I had crossed the wasteland of financial disillusionment, both personal and cultural. Now, for the first time, I was conscious of a connection to a spiritual source, something greater than the material world, something invisible but intelligent that seemed to be directing the circus of human affairs. I still didn't understand the relationship between this unseen hand and true wealth, but at least I was less worried about the split and more genuinely confident about a coming resolution.

At the age of thirty-three, I arrived at JFK Airport in New York with thirty dollars in my pocket. I hailed a taxi, took it to a friend's apartment in Manhattan, and when I read twenty-four dollars on the meter, gave the driver my three tens and told him to keep the change.

I lived from hand-to-mouth for five years, never having missed a meal or not having a roof over my head. In fact, my years without money were some of the most prosperous ones. I always seemed to be surrounded by wealth and now was supported by the abundance. I lived in San Francisco and Santa Fe, and everywhere I went I had wealthy friends whose generosity amazed me. I lived well, often rent-free in luxury dwellings, sometimes in cramped communal quarters. Wherever I was, however, I felt that I belonged there for a reason, and even though the prosperity I lived in was not "mine," the concept of "mine" itself was taking on new meaning. I was beginning to think that the entire world was mine in a sense. The veil of separation between myself and the rest of the world was lifting. And I was realizing

that material possessions were limited compared to the unlimited, "unownable" wealth of the universe given us.

My career changed almost with what seemed like a will of its
own. Even though I had won a playwriting award from the National Endowment for the Arts and had begun to establish myself
as a director, my interest turned from the results to the process,
from the show to the rehearsal. I had always been fascinated by
the depth of self-discovery the good actors reach while construct-
ing the actions that become their characters. But now my fascina-
tion was all-consuming and I didn't want to be concerned about
the end product at all. At the same time, my journey was taking
me towards further self-discovery, beginning with yoga and meditation, continuing with self-help seminars, and climaxing with
rebirthing.

It seemed like the energy I had invested into rebellion in the
sixties was now being funneled into a spiritual quest. I examined
the inner demons that I once projected as political and parental
enemies. I was searching for peace but addicted to conflict. I studied my birth script and my unconscious life scenarios, and understood that my life had been a self-fulfilling prophecy. I realized
that the movies of my subconscious mind were the dramas, soap
operas, and situation comedies of my life. And I saw myself as
the author, producer, director, and leading man of my own show.

The more I shared my realizations with others, the more I
naturally took on the role of seminar leader, consultant, and healing coach...and prospered. This took me by surprise because I
never expected to make money on a spiritual path. Nevertheless,
I was learning to receive more of everything—love, energy, money,
whatever—and I couldn't do a damn thing about it.

Not that I minded. It was ironic that after all my conflict
about money, it would come to me so easily. At first I did find it
hard to accept. All my thoughts of unworthiness, guilt, family
loyalties, and needing to struggle to justify my existence were be-

ing confronted by newfound but undeniable experiences of the opposite. Gradually, I surrendered to my financial destiny as being part of my spiritual journey. I realized that there was a unity behind all diversity and that my previous addiction to fragmenting the universe was simply the result of being lost in my own innocent perceptions. I understood that love and money, work and play, career and family spring from one source which supports all life. Moreover, I came to believe that all of us have a purpose, that what we love to do most is our reason for being here, and that we would make the greatest contribution if we created a sane economy based on love and talent rather than the schizophrenic one we have embraced for far too long.

I think that many of us undergo a similar financial and personal evolution. At first we think we have everything, and indeed we do. Then we learn from our parents, teachers, culture and experiences that some of us have more than others, that the source is outside ourselves, and that we are just little insignificant beings in a vast universe. We learn that to succeed we have to struggle in a rat race; sacrifice what we want for what we need; and live in fear of scarcity, loss, and destitution. Perhaps we become financial atheists, thinking that there is no spirit other than our own will and that there's nothing reliable in life except ourselves. Some of us succeed on this path, but more often than not, we reach a point where our internal satisfaction falls short of our external success. Some find the inner wealth without the outer accoutrements. But if we keep on going, we expand into a deeper and greater sense of wealth. We come to see that the spiritual source is both inside and outside us, that it is the connective fabric in which all of life is woven, and that the great challenge of life is to both acknowledge and tap this universal abundance for our individual betterment, the collective well-being, and the health of our living planet.

The days of divide and conquer, exploit and pillage, are rapidly disappearing, obviously based on false premises which inevitably lead to diminishing returns. The spirit of true wealth is calling to us. Nothing less will suffice. We all want to wake up to a world of wealth, and that world is truly ours for the taking...and the giving.

It is my prayer that this book will be part of your wake-up call.

Bob Mandel has been a pioneer for self-improvement nearly twenty years. He is well known as both a writer and group facilitator for his clarity, intuition, humor, wisdom, and compassion. Currently, he is the co-owner of two educational seminar companies, LRT International and ISLP Inc. Bob lives in rural Connecticut and divides his time between teaching worldwide, conducting long-term programs and celebrating his loving relationships with family and friends.

For further information about the Loving Relationships Training (LRT) and International Seminars Leadership Programs (ISLP), write to Bob at P.O. Box 1465, Washington, CT 06793.

Other Books and Tapes by Bob Mandel

Books:

Money Mantras
Open Heart Therapy
Two Hearts Are Better Than One
Heart Over Heels
Birth & Relationships (with Sondra Ray)

Tapes:

"Money Mantras"
"God Provides"
"Peace With Passion"
"Rebirth" by Sagitarius
"I Am As God Created Me" by Grace
"Sexual Love" by Sagitarius

For information about these and other products contact
LRT INTERNATIONAL, P.O. Box 1465, Washington, CT 06793,
telephone 1-800-INTL-LRT.